You Can Do It!
A Step by Step Guide on
How to Achieve Your Dreams

by

Shelley Dudley

authorHOUSE®

AuthorHouse™
1663 Liberty Drive
Bloomington, IN 47403
www.authorhouse.com
Phone: 1-800-839-8640

First published by AuthorHouse   08/01/2011

ISBN: 978-1-4567-8820-9 (sc)

Printed in the United States of America

Dedication

For my Dad, who has always believed in me, supported me, and loved me, in countless ways. Thank you, Dad!

And for my very special friends, Gayness, Rodney, Arecha, Carol, and Kim. Your wisdom and guidance have helped me to turn my own life around and make my own dreams come true.

And for that very special man who inspires me to be my very best and highest self. Thank you, James.

"Your battles inspired me -
not the obvious material battles but
those that were fought and
won behind your forehead"
James Joyce

Table of Contents

Introduction... 13

Chapter One - Finding Your Passion...................................... 15

Chapter Two - Creating Your Goals....................................... 33

Chapter Three - Develop a Plan of Action.............................. 55

Chapter Four - The Power of Focus....................................... 69

Chapter Five - Maintaining Motivation.................................... 95

Chapter Six - Overcoming Barriers.. 107

Chapter Seven - Using Your Intuition 137

Chapter Eight - The Way Forward.. 161

BIBLIOGRAPHY... 169

Acknowledgements

I have not attempted to cite in the text all of the authorities and sources consulted in the preparation of this book. To do so would require more space and time than is available. Scores of people contributed to this book and in writing it, it is evident that I am standing on the shoulders of giants.

I am humbled and grateful to those that were bold enough and brave enough to pioneer new ground in the fields of psycho-cybernetics, positive psychology, self development, quantum physics, and other disciplines that have contributed greatly in helping man's soul to soar.

Having said that, I would be remiss if I did not acknowledge the exceptional insight and contributions of a select handful of people. Therefore, I wish to personally thank Jim Stovall for his very humble heart, his great contribution, and for opening countless doors; Brian Johnson, Bill Bartmann, Tracy Trost, Cecily McArthur, Veronica Robertson, and Glenn Fisher, for their openness in their interviews and for sharing their lives and learnings with the world. All of you are owed a debt of gratitude for your honesty and willingness to give to others.

Disclaimer

This book is designed to provide information on self-empowerment and self-improvement. It is sold with the understanding that the publisher and author are not engaged in rendering legal, accounting or other professional services. If legal or other expert assistance is required, the services of a competent professional should be sought.

It is not the purpose of this book to reprint all the information that is otherwise available to the public on this subject, but instead to complement, amplify and supplement other texts.

You are urged to read all the available material, learn as much as possible about self-improvement, and tailor the information to your individual needs. For more information, see the many resources in the Bibliography.

Self-improvement is not an overnight project. Anyone who decides to stretch beyond their current boundaries, to grow and change must expect to invest time and effort into it.

Every effort has been made to make this book as complete and as accurate as possible. However, there *may be mistakes*, both typographical and in content. Therefore, this text should be used only as a general guide and not as the ultimate source on self-development. Furthermore, this book contains information on self-improvement that is current only up to the printing date.

The purpose of this book is to educate and entertain. The author and publisher shall have neither liability nor responsibility to any person or entity with respect to any loss or damage caused, or alleged to have been caused, directly or indirectly, by the information contained in this book.

If you do not wish to be bound by the above, you may return this book to the publisher for a full refund.

FOREWORD

As you read these pages, I want to compliment you on engaging in the most common activity among successful people. The most significant, consistent trait among people who achieve in business and life is that of consistently reading motivational and instructional material. Each page you turn in this book confirms the fact that you are one step closer to who you want to be and where you want to be.

I am very proud that Shelley asked me to be a part of this exciting project. She and I met through an international teleconference where I was speaking. Shelley took the initiative to contact me and to ask me to be a part of this effort. I felt honored to offer this foreword and to be interviewed for one of the chapters. The caliber and quality of the leaders you will learn from in this book is a tribute to Shelley's commitment to bring you the best practical information with real world examples.

If you want to succeed in life you've got to accept counsel and direction from those who are successful. When it's all said and done in our world, there is a lot said and very little done. Never take advice from someone who does not have what you want. Talk is cheap and action is rare. All of us have a million reasons not to succeed in life, and only our passion and commitment as a reason to overcome.

There is probably no one you will ever meet less qualified to be a success than me. When I think of myself as an Emmy Award Winning founder of a television network, the author of over a dozen books, several of which have become major motion pictures, one of the most sought-after arena and convention speakers or just someone that Shelley thought enough of to be a part of this project, I am amazed.

As a blind person myself, I know what it's like to have no expectations of success and to be surrounded by people who have no expectations for my achievement. Through countless audio books featuring people like those you will learn about in these pages, I formed my own dream team of success. I determined to listen to people who had been where I wanted to be and believed I could do it, too. This is what I desire for you. I do not know your name or the circumstances that have connected you and I through this book, but the one thing I know about you is that you were created with a big dream and a passion for this life.

I am convinced that that big dream would not have been put inside of you if you did not have the capacity to achieve it. Shelley and the other thought-leaders in this book will convince you of that. But all of us still deal with doubt and adversity. Any time you question whether the principles in these chapters apply to you and you need someone to believe in you, please call me at (918) 627-1000 or email jim@jimstovall.com. I want to join Shelley and the others involved in this project in becoming a partner in your success. Any time you doubt that commitment or your own capacity to succeed, simply email or call me. I look forward to your success and to someday reading your story in another of Shelley's books.

Jim Stovall, 2010

Introduction

Sometimes in life you are drawn to a book or a person, a movie or an event, because that person or thing holds something you need: a message, a lesson, or something that will help you sort a problem you've been trying to solve. I believe this is often the case and it may be why you've chosen to read this book.

Whatever the case, I expect there will be much of great value in it for you.

Whether you've had a tough life and wish to totally turn your path around or perhaps you're just tired of the repetition of the day-in-day-out treadmill, or maybe you've been working toward a goal, but you feel stuck; in any event, you were born to be more and are destined to achieve greatness and this book will help you to get there. In short, if you want to 'up your game,' this is the book for you!

In the coming chapters, you will learn how to clarify your dreams and goals, those that may seem pie-in-the-sky, those that scare you, and those that appear to be more realistic. You will also set into motion a plan of action for achieving those goals, gaining some very good insight and skills along the way. You will learn why you've 'failed' at past attempts to achieve your dreams and how you can overcome both small hurdles and BIG barriers that might stand in your way. You will stretch yourself and you will develop momentum. Your motivation will be high. In short, you will learn how to turn your life around and achieve your dreams!

You will also learn from others who have walked a mile in your shoes; people who have been where you are and have turned their own lives around to achieve greatness and realize their own goals. You will not only learn from their mistakes and their wisdom, but you will be inspired by their achievements and the abundance they've brought into their own lives and the lives of others. You will learn in their own words how they've achieved their dreams.

So without delay, let's begin . . . .

Chapter One - Finding Your Passion

"Insanity is doing the same thing
in the same way and
expecting a different outcome. "
Old Chinese Proverb

It is not uncommon for a person to wake up one morning, unexcited about his life, knowing that today will be exactly like yesterday and the week before that, and tomorrow, and next week, and all the foreseeable weeks to come. It is not uncommon at this point in life to ask, "What is it all for? Why am I doing this?"

Viktor Frankl, in his great book *Man's Search for Meaning* said that, "Ultimately, man should not ask what the meaning of his life is, but rather must recognize that it is he who is asked. In a word, each man is questioned by life; and he can only answer to life by answering for his own life."

If you're switched on, questioning what it's all for can be a defining moment . . . a turning point for you. It was for me. And it was how I came to be writing this book for you at this present time.

It is normal for a person to float through life without truly knowing what their purpose is or what it is that they want to achieve. It certainly was my own story.

Without any direction, we take the path of least resistance and wind up wherever the current takes us. If we are incredibly lucky, the current may take us for a peaceful ride over smooth water. If we are not so lucky (and this happens more often than not), we may be dashed upon the rocks, never knowing what hit us or where we've landed and why.

Just think about what would happen if you got into your car and you intended to take a very long journey, but you didn't have a destination in mind. You would waste a lot of time, money and energy just driving around in circles. And, sure, you would end up somewhere, but would it be someplace good? Would it be where you wanted to go? How many mishaps would you have along the way, just because you had no plan to follow?

We all have a destination in life - someplace that we will end up at the finish of our journey. Stephen R Covey said, "If the ladder is not leaning against the right wall, every step we take just gets us to the wrong place faster". How true that is.

How much more fun is our journey if we've pre-planned our destination and a rough route to get there, with a bit of planned site-seeing along the way! Life is exactly the same as our vacation example.

When we have a designated goal in mind, a good idea how we're going to get there, and we remain flexible enough to adjust course along the way, we're much more likely to land at our expected destination and we're much more likely to enjoy the journey.

The hidden danger lies, though, in choosing the wrong destination. What do I mean?

What if you've always dreamed of being an artist? Of sharing your passion with the world through paint on canvas?

"Oh no, dear," your mother said. "However will you feed yourself? You don't want to wind up a poor starving artist, do you?"

"Why don't you become an accountant like your Uncle Stanley? Settle down and get a REAL JOB," your father advised.

And so . . . having taken your family's advice on board, you put your dream of becoming a painter on the back burner and chose a more practical vocation . . . one that was 9-5 and offered a miniscule but steady paycheck or, if the paycheck was larger, the hours were awful and either way most likely offered a life of quiet desperation. After all, they had a good point, didn't they? And they always have your best interests at heart, right?

For me it was a dream of traveling the world. I wanted to see as many countries and experience as many cultures as I possibly could in this lifetime. I decided the best way to do this was to become a political ambassador (don't ask me why) and with that in mind, I set my 17 year old heart on attending the foremost university to prepare me for my chosen career. Unfortunately, my mother (who would much rather have her children near home) took one look at the cost of tuition and the fact that my chosen university was three thousand miles away and replied a flat no. My dreams were immediately dashed. Instead of standing my ground, I allowed her to talk me into attending a local college where I "could study something more practical," as my mother suggested, and I gave up my dream of traveling the world, while righting the world's political injustices.

But what did I do in that moment? I allowed someone else (as good as their intentions were) to choose my life's path for me. I denied my own heart and my own imagination in favor of the desires of well-meaning friends and family. How many times can you deny your own spirit before it slowly starts to wither and die?

And how often throughout our lives do we do this very thing without even realizing? We allow others to choose our occupation for us when we heed their advice to 'be practical' and 'get a real job.' We allow others to choose our life's partner for us when we marry someone our parents would approve, instead of the 'outsider' we fell in love with. We do what's considered safe and we go along with the current, until one day we wake up, dashed upon the rocks, asking ourselves, "What is it all for? Why am I doing this?"

Sometimes it's not the well-meaning advice of others that has led us astray, but our own fear of making mistakes and our desire to play it safe.

Sir Ken Robinson commented on the nature of the world's school systems when he said that children start life willing to take a chance, without the fear of making mistakes or being wrong. However, "by the time they get to be adults, most kids have lost that capacity. They have become frightened of being wrong. And we run our companies this way. We stigmatize mistakes. And we now have national education systems where mistakes are the worst thing you can make. And the result is that we are educating people out of their creative capacities."

As told by Daniel Goleman, Howard Gardner, the Harvard psychologist who came up with the idea of 'multiple intelligences,' expanded this idea: "'The time has come,' Gardner told me, 'to broaden our notion of the spectrum of talents. The single most important contribution education can make to a child's development is to help him toward a field where his talents best suit him, where he will be satisfied and competent. We've completely lost sight of that. Instead we subject everyone to an education where, if you succeed, you will be best suited to be a college professor. And we evaluate everyone along the way according to whether they meet that narrow standard of success. We should spend less time ranking children and more time helping them to identify their natural competencies and gifts, and cultivate those. There are hundreds and hundreds of ways to succeed and many, many, many different abilities that will help get you there.'"

Jack Canfield agreed. He stated, "I think there's too much emphasis placed on learning things by rote that you don't really care about. So what happens to students in school is that they eventually lose interest in learning, because they've been forced to learn the required courses, rather than pursing their passion."

And His Holiness the 14th Dalai Lama of Tibet said, "Everyone, everywhere, is basically the same in wanting happiness and not to suffer."

So how do we counteract the fact that we've allowed everyone else to choose our life's path for us? How do we turn the course of our life around and put it on a path of our own choosing? How do we stop suffering, as the Dalai Lama said, and regain that passion?

For that, we need to fire up our imaginations. "In imagination," Mark Victor Hansen said, "there's no limitation."

Stephen R. Covey, when discussing the ladder we mentioned previously, said that one should always "begin with the end in mind".

So, I want you to imagine you are attending a funeral. As you enter the church, you take a seat at the back and look around. You see some people that are familiar to you. A priest enters the front of the church and stands at the pulpit.

"We are gathered here today," he says, "to honor the life of (insert your name here)."

You realize that you are seeing a fore-glimpse of your own funeral.

"It is only fitting," the priest continues, "that those who loved (insert your name here) most should share their thoughts and memories. Who would like to go first?" You see your life partner of many years stand up to speak. You see that (s)he is teary-eyed, but smiling, as (s)he recalls some of his/her happiest memories of you.

What does (s)he say about your relationship and the kind of partner you were? What do your children say about the kind of father or mother you've been? What do your co-workers and business colleagues say about your work ethics? What do your friends say about the type of friend you've been to them? And finally, what do the local charities say about you?

Is it a eulogy you are proud to hear? Is it one that could be better?

Incidentally, if attending your own funeral is a bit too morbid, you can always imagine that you are attending your own 100th birthday party and that everyone is there to help you celebrate. Their speeches and memories are to honor your life's work. Do you like what you hear? Take some time right now to vividly imagine one scenario or the other.

As Stephen Covey says, "Begin with the end in mind." Get a clear picture in your head of how you would like your eulogy (or honorary speeches) to sound. Take a moment now and put this book down to actually write that out on paper.

I'll share with you my own, but it will by no means be the same for you. There is no "right" or "wrong" here. Each person's vision of their own life is going to be as individual as they are. What is your highest ideal for yourself? What do you wish your life to have said about you? My own ideal goes something like this:

My life partner starts off by saying, "Thank you all for coming today. It is easy to see how well-loved Shelley is (was) by the vast number of people that are in attendance. That's also a testament to how many lives she has touched.

Shelley's not always had an easy life and there were times when she compared herself to a planarian when it came to learning, but she was steadfast and adamant that she no longer wanted to settle for ordinary and that she was determined to turn the course of her life around. And she did . . . in a big way! Never one to do things by halves, Shelley traveled the world, spreading a message of hope and teaching people of all different cultures that we are essentially the same in all wanting to be happy. She shared with them her message of how to achieve happiness, sometimes sharing the stage with the most influential people in the world - notables like Bob Proctor, Jack Canfield, Brian Johnson, Vishen Lahkiani, Jim Stovall, Sir Richard Branson, and the Dalai Lama. She won many awards for her speeches and her message was heard the world over.

Shelley also wrote many books and, as you well know, many of those went on to become best-sellers and have been published in many languages and countries.

Shelley has (had) a big heart and shared lots of love with her family and friends and she thoroughly enjoyed having them around her."

One of my business partners then stands and says, "Shelley is (was) an astute business woman. She was strong in integrity and while she drove a hard bargain in every deal, she always sought win-win outcomes and gave so much of herself that she couldn't help becoming wealthy. While not all of her investments paid off, she learned quickly and put her money where it was best used wisely and, as a result, she has built a vast financial empire, leaving a strong legacy behind."

A representative from one of the many charities in the room stands and says, "But don't think that Shelley was a greedy person. Not at all. I speak for all the charitable organizations represented here tonight and we would say that Shelley was generous to a fault, giving away an incredible amount of her income to better the lives of children and animals in various parts of the world. She has made a significant impact and, speaking for my own charity here, were it not for Shelley's help, the people of X village would have neither safe drinking water nor a modern school for their children. Because of Shelley, many of the people in this village have meaningful work - work that causes them to feel significant, important, and connected to the rest of the world. The work that she has started will be carried on for many generations to come."

Your speech or eulogy will likely be very different from mine. You are an individual and your vision for your life will be as unique as you are. I offer one additional example before I ask you to take a moment to write your own:

The priest stands at the pulpit and says, "We are gathered today to honor the life of Jacob 'Jake' Flynn. Jake was a good man, one who gave of himself unselfishly when he served on behalf of his country during World War II, receiving the Purple Heart for his bravery in combat. After returning from the war, Jake became a mechanic and devoted himself to being the very best mechanic he knew how to be, often able to diagnose a problem others had failed to find. His customers loved him well and many have stated that there was no finer or fairer mechanic in this part of the country.

He leaves behind a beautiful wife, the apple of his eye and the heart of his heart, a woman who loves him dearly and was devoted to him for better than 60 years. It is a testament to Jake that he loved her more on the day of his death than he did on their wedding day and that every day he devoted himself more and more to their relationship.

Jake also leaves behind three loving children and six beautiful grandchildren, in whom he had much pride. He spent much time with his family and he instilled his values and integrity in his children and the legacy he leaves behind will carry on in the generations to come. Jake had much to be proud of.

Although not one for attending church, Jake was an honest man who was always fair in his dealings with others and he always had a knack for bringing out the best in people. He was also a generous man who enjoyed helping others where he could. For 25 years he voluntarily drove the only ambulance in the region and asked for nothing in return. There are many who will miss his kind heart."

What is it that you aspire to do, be, and have in this life? What legacy do you wish to leave behind? Take a moment now and write down your thoughts in this regard.

I'm going to assume you've taken the time to do the last exercise and that you're ready to continue onward now. While it was likely useful to you in helping you to crystallize the direction you wish your life's path to take and what some of your deep-rooted values might be, we still really haven't talked much about passion.

Neil Diamond said, "It's all about finding out who you are and what your passion is, which for me is music." Abraham Maslow stated that an individual's passion may "take the form of the desire to be an excellent parent, in another it may be expressed athletically, and in still another it may be expressed in painting pictures or in inventing things."

What is it that you have a gift or a talent for? What have you always dreamed of doing, being, or having in your life? (For me it was travel: seeing new places, speaking new languages, and experiencing new cultures.) What is it that gets you excited about life, causes enthusiasm to just boil over when you talk about it or think about it? What is it that really makes you want to jump out of bed in the morning, on fire with the joy of life? In order to answer this, you may have to think back to when you were young, before your dreams were beaten down by loving, well-meaning, family, friends, school professors, and authorities in your life.

Take a moment now to put the book down and really introspect. Take some quiet time to really look inside yourself at who you are, what your values are, what you believe in, and what's important to you. When you come back to the book I'm going to ask you, "What is your passion?" Don't be concerned with whether you think you can have, do, or be it - or not. At this stage in the game, that is not the question and we will address that later.

Walt Disney said, "If you can dream it, you can achieve it" and Richard Bach concurred, when he said, "You are never given a *dream* without also being given the power to make it true."

Assume for now that there is NO WAY you can fail to have, do, or be this thing your heart desires. What is that thing? Ask yourself in your meditation, "If I knew that I was GUARANTEED to SUCCEED, what is it that I would do, be, or have in my life that I don't have (or have enough of) right now?" Don't limit yourself. Make a whole list of "to dos," "to bes," and "to haves," as many as you can think of that you truly desire! Put the book down and do that.

Are you back now? How did it go? Did you take some time to quietly meditate and look inside your heart and mind at what's really important to you? Good. Maslow said, "Musicians must make music, artists must paint, poets must write if they are to be ultimately at peace with themselves. What human beings can be, they must be. They must be true to their own nature. This need we may call self-actualization . . . It refers to man's desire for self-fulfillment, namely to the tendency for him to become actually what he is potentially: to become everything one is capable of becoming."

Now that you've had a bit of time to think about it, write down the top five to ten 'things' that came out of your introspection. What are the top ten things that are most important to you - things you are passionate about? Possible examples:

1. I love travel,
2. I am passionate about art (or music or sports),
3. I enjoy working with my hands, doing intricate detailed work,
4. My kids mean everything to me,
5. I love helping people,

. . . and so on. If there are not ten on your list, don't worry. A list of less is easier to work with. If there are more than ten things on your list, you will need to narrow it down. The best way to do that is to randomly choose one of the items on your list. Now compare it with another item on your list. Ask yourself, "If I could only have, do, or be one of these two items in my life and had to get rid of the other, which would it be?" Keep the one that is most important to you and that now becomes your model for comparison. Keep comparing and asking yourself if you had to get rid of one, which would it be, until you've narrowed your list to ten items. Now take a good hard look at those ten items that are on your list. Let's narrow it down to five. By doing that, we will really be getting at the core of who you are, what your inner values are, and what drives your passion.

So take a good look at your list again and rework the exercise. If you could only keep one item on the list and had to get rid of all the rest, what one item would it be? What does this say about you and what you value? I didn't ask what the rest of the world would think of this item being number one on your list. Forget the rest of the world for now! And especially forget those loving and well-meaning nay-sayers who always have your best interests at heart! What does your choice tell you about your own values? What does it tell you about who you are?

Now, if you were allowed to add back in one more item (and ONLY one more item) to your list, what one item would you claim back? What does this item say about you?

Continue asking yourself these questions until your list contains five things you are passionate about and you are certain these are the five items that make the truest statement about who you really are.

Now copy this list several times and post it in several prominent places so that you will see it on a daily basis - the bathroom mirror, the refrigerator, the back of the front door, etc. Your awakening has begun.

Perhaps it's not the case that you don't know what your passions are. Maybe you've known all along but just don't get enough time, money, or other resources to devote to them or you feel like life's circumstances have pulled you away from them.

Maxwell Maltz said that to deny our true selves (our passions) is to live in constant frustration which is tantamount to taking a knife and stabbing ourselves in the back. Very vivid picture . . . and apt metaphor.

So if this is the case for you, I have one more exercise for you to do, called the Wheel of Life. This exercise is designed to help you restore balance in your life and it looks something like the example below:

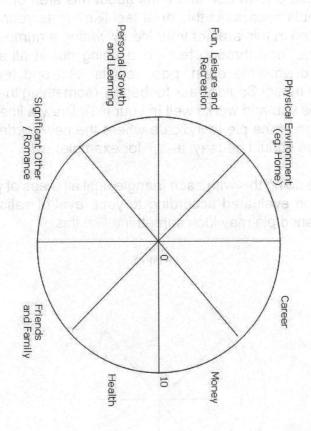

Get out a blank sheet of paper and draw a large circle upon it. Divide that circle into at least eight areas (more if required or desired), so that it winds up looking like a pie. Assign a title to each wedge of pie. These titles are going to relate, first of all, to your top three passions, if not all five (so one triangle of pie for each of your top three passions) and to all the other things in your life that demand your precious time or drain your energy (or give you energy). Use more than eight wedges of pie, if needed. The central point of the pie is marked zero ('0') and the outer edge of the pie is marked ten ('10').

Now that all the wedges are labeled according to your own life, choose one wedge and think about this area of your life. What would success in this area feel like? Rate your level of satisfaction in this area of your life by writing a number in the pie wedge, one through ten - one being not at all satisfied (energy drain, time drain, poor results, etc) and ten being 'Over the moon! Couldn't ask for better!' (something that totally energizes you and works well in your life). Draw a line across the wedge of the pie to indicate where the new border of the pie wedge should be (say, at a 7 for example).

Continue doing this with each triangle until all areas of your life have been evaluated according to your level of satisfaction. Your finished pie may look something like this:

EXAMPLE

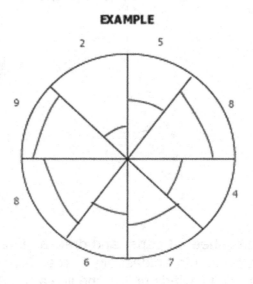

Now, looking at your wheel and each of the elements in it, ask yourself these questions:

1. Are there any surprises for you?
2. How do you feel about your life as you look at your wheel?
3. How do you currently spend time in these areas?
4. How would you LIKE to spend time in these areas?
5. Which of these elements would you most like to improve?
6. How could you make space for these changes?
7. Can you effect the necessary changes on your own?
8. What help and cooperation from others might you need?
9. What would make that area of your life a score of 10?
10. What would a score of 10 feel like?

By the time you have worked your way through this exercise you should have a very good sense of the various elements of your life and how balanced they are in relation to each other, according to your own values. You should have a good feel for which areas of your life are draining your energy and where changes can be made. You should also have a good feel for those areas of your life that fill you with energy and you might be starting to sense how you can bring more of those into your life.

Remember what Stephen R. Covey said? "We may be very busy, we may be very efficient, but we will also be truly effective only when we begin with the end in mind."

Hopefully this chapter's exercises have helped you to visualize how your life is now in relation to how you would like your life to be and where you can begin to think about making positive changes to bring the two into closer alignment with each other. The exercises in this chapter should also have helped you define some of your deepest core values and identify some of your burning passions. As we continue through the rest of the book, this is the foundation we will be working from.

I am inspired by the story of Brian Johnson, a man whose story is similar to my own in many respects.

Raised in a conservative, predominantly Catholic family, as a young man he wanted to make his family proud and enrolled at university to study psychology, where he received a tiny inkling that he might have a passion for learning what makes people tick.

However, upon graduating UCLA, he felt the need to embark upon a 'respectable' profession and he went to work for Arthur Andersen, one of 'the big five' accounting firms (before it imploded in the Enron scandal).

Raised by a mother who instilled in him that he had gifts to give to the world and that he was a part of something greater than himself, young Brian knew that someday he would be great. It appeared to all the world that he had life by the tail.
It was during his first week of work, however, that Brian became literally nauseous and knew in his heart that accounting was not who he was. Driving home from work one night across the bridge on the L.A. freeway, Brian pulled over, got out of his car, and while traffic was whizzing by, literally threw up on the side of the road. He had a deep sense that accounting "just wasn't me and I was imagining my life ten, twenty years forward and it was literally making me nauseous."

Having no idea what he wanted to do with his life, but knowing that accounting wasn't it, he enrolled in one of the U.S.'s leading law schools and thought that he would become a great lawyer with a six figure income. Brian's never been short on drive.

He had been studying only a semester when he realized that law was definitely not who he is either and subsequently dropped out of school at the age of 23.

In the depths of despair at this point, Brian became disillusioned with trying to "do the right thing and impress other people" with his choice of career, and he burned his résumé. "I had no compass and didn't know how I was going to figure it out," he said.

Still having no clue what he wanted to do with his life or where his passions lie, he started coaching a little league team of nine and ten year old baseball players, which was something he enjoyed doing and gave him the opportunity to fulfill a bit of the upbringing he had which taught him to give back to the world. "In hindsight," Brian said, "It was my little bit of Joseph Campbell's bliss."

At the same time he began doing some consulting work for Arthur Andersen, guiding the company through the maze of new technology. "I saw that the web was really growing in 1998 and saw the potential of databases" Brian said, "and I realized that it would only be a short period of time before every team and league, every kid and family who played sports would be using the web for everything and I created my first business out of that."

Brian raised five million dollars and won awards with that business "and did some amazing things in the dot com boom that I never could have predicted when I left law school. And by just following what little bit of bliss that I had in working with these kids, this extraordinary idea came to fruition."

"I've seen that pattern happen again and again in my life," Brian said, "when, if I just trust myself and follow my heart and work diligently, great things happen that I never could have predicted would happen."

Today Brian lives his passion without hesitation and follows his bliss in being a great philosopher. He studies the profound writings of sages throughout history (and in modern times) and Brian condenses those learnings into bite-size and manageable 'big ideas' that busy people can read, watch, or listen to in twenty minutes or less. His creations can be found at http://tinyurl.com/34vsmm2 and I would highly recommend giving them a listen. It takes only a few seconds hearing Brian speak about his life and his work to realize how passionate he is.

Brian's big message? "You can do it too! Just listen to your heart and follow your bliss!"

Chapter Two - Creating Your Goals

You control your future, your destiny.
What you think about comes about. By
recording your dreams and goals on paper, you
set in motion the process of becoming the person
you most want to be.

Mark Victor Hansen

Science has established a clear link between goal setting and achievement. According to Jay Rifenbary, Yale University graduates were surveyed in 1953 and then again 20 years later. The outcomes of the research showed that 3% of those graduates had generated more wealth than the other 97%; this same 3% enjoyed better health and experienced more successful relationships.

None of the usual factors accounted for this difference: background, parental wealth, degree studied, gender, or career selected. The only difference that could be found was that all of the 3% had set goals for themselves in the 1950s, whilst the majority of the 97% had not. You will find that having clearly defined goals offers your life a sense of purpose and direction.

Additionally, something happens when we actually put pen to paper to write out our goals. We turn our thoughts into something tangible. We can actually see our goal, feel it, smell it, taste it, touch it! The goal is no longer just a thought; it has now become something that motivates us and creates a gut feeling inside.

Even the act of using the eye in coordination with the hand holding the pen makes a much stronger impression on our mind as we write out our goal. When we read and re-read that phrase or sentence, the impression on the mind becomes even deeper.

In the last chapter we worked through some exercises that should have given you a clearer idea of the general direction you wish to move in your life. If you're like me, you're probably now itching to set some goals and get started. However, before we do that, we want to make sure that our goals will actually be achievable, that we will attain victory. After all, we don't want to fall flat on our faces, do we?

"That's easy!" you may say. "Just set small easily achieved goals." And you would be right; that's one way to go about it. However, think back to a time when you really, really wanted something badly. For me, it was my first car. My single-parent mother didn't have the money to go out and buy me one, so if I wanted it, it was up to me to figure out a way to get it. So I found myself a job in the local cinema, serving popcorn, and I worked hard on top of going to school and I scrimped and saved for over a year until I had enough money to buy my first car. I guarantee you it was the ugliest thing on four wheels, mustard yellow, but the immense excitement and pride I felt when I handed over the cash I'd saved and I took possession of the keys was enormous.

Was it an easy goal? No. I was not allowed to let my grade point average slip at school, so I'd had to stay up until the wee hours many nights after work to study for an exam or do homework for the next day. I had to forego social outings with my friends in order to be at work and I always smelled like popcorn grease no matter how often I showered. On Friday and Saturday nights the popular kids would bring their dates to the cinema and I would die of embarrassment, wishing the trap door in the floor would swallow me up, as I stood there in my geeky, grease-stained uniform asking them if they wanted some popcorn to go with their Coke.

Was it worth it? Absolutely! I had to stretch myself and change the way I thought in order to reach that goal. I had to make some sacrifices. But the enormous feeling of freedom that car gave me, being able to drive myself wherever I wanted to go . . . once I had it, I wouldn't have traded it for anything!

It is likely that you yourself have had a similar experience - one where you had to reach in order to achieve something. How did you feel when you attained your goal? Was it worth the stretch?

Mihaly Csikszentmihalyi stated, "The optimal state of inner experience is one in which there is *order in consciousness*. This happens when psychic energy - or attention - is invested in realistic goals, and when skills match the opportunities for action. The pursuit of a goal brings order in awareness because a person must concentrate attention on the task at hand and momentarily forget everything else. These periods of struggling to overcome challenges are what people find to be the most enjoyable of their lives. A person who has achieved control over psychic energy and has invested it in consciously chosen goals cannot help but grow into a more complex being. By stretching skills, by reaching toward higher challenges, such a person becomes an increasingly extraordinary individual."

I like the concise way that Robert Allen, author of *Creating Wealth* and *Nothing Down*, put it. He said, "Everything you want is just outside your comfort zone." In other words, you're going to have to get off the sofa to get it!

It's a funny thing about goals. When they fall inside our comfort zone, we don't tend to appreciate them at all, because we haven't had to work for them. For example, let's say that you see that you are getting low on milk, so you put it on your 'to-do' list to go to the grocery store and get some milk. That is your goal. It is likely that beyond that, you don't give it another thought, neither in the planning of how to get it, nor in the actual attainment of it. You won't do a big victory dance in the grocery store parking lot or buy a bottle of champagne to celebrate the fact that you've achieved your goal of buying some milk. It is the same with any goal that falls inside your comfort zone.

"Well then," you say, "the answer is obviously to set goals that are well outside your comfort zone, right?" I can see you are astute and catch on quickly.

We do need to be careful, though, that we don't set our goals too far outside of our comfort zone so as to cause panic, else we will never even attempt to achieve them.

For example, if I were your boss at work and I said that, as a teambuilding exercise, we were all going skydiving tomorrow (and by the way, this teambuilding exercise is mandatory), how would you feel? For some, this idea would be just fine, but for others it would definitely be a no-go! There are two elements to this goal that might be distasteful.

The first is that it is a goal that I've set for you, not a goal you've set for yourself. Any goals that are imposed from outside and not adopted as inner-felt desires are going to have a low motivation factor and the only reason we attempt to achieve these at all is because, either we desire the carrot at the end of the donkey-stick, or we do not wish to disappoint or incur the wrath of whomever has imposed the target upon us. Either way, there is a low chance of success with this type of goal. If we don't 'own' a goal, then we are likely to lack the real drive, passion, and commitment necessary to achieve it.

The second thing about this goal of skydiving that might cause a person to say, "No way, Jose!" is that it may be so far outside their comfort zone that it sends them straight into the panic zone. When we move into the panic zone, we can experience many uncomfortable feelings such as anxiety, nausea, tension and stress, nervousness, memory loss, and energy loss.

Ultimately, what we're aiming for is a good balance between what our skills and abilities can handle and what we have to grow and learn new skills to achieve. When our goals fall into this area, it is called being in the stretch zone and always this is the zone we will be in when we achieve a state of FLOW.

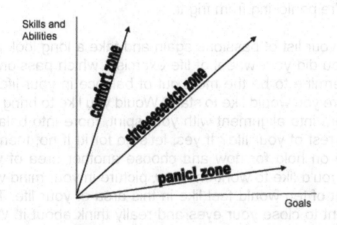

Csikszentmihalyi states that, "In all the activities people in our study reported engaging in, enjoyment comes at a very specific point: whenever the opportunities for action perceived by the individual are equal to his or her capabilities. Playing tennis, for instance, is not enjoyable if the two opponents are mismatched. The less skilled player will feel anxious, and the better player will feel bored. The same is true for every other activity . . . Enjoyment appears at the boundary between boredom and anxiety, when the challenges are just balanced with the person's capacity to act."

This is the heart of flow: We need to create goals where our skills match our challenges. If our skills are far greater than the challenge, we are going to get bored. If the challenge is far greater than our skills, we become anxious and stressed. When our skills match the challenge? Enter flow!

Brian Tracy said, "Move out of your comfort zone. You can only grow if you are willing to feel awkward and uncomfortable when you try something new."

So with that in mind, let's begin to think about some goals that will make you stretch a bit - just enough to cause you to do that public victory dance upon achievement but not so much that you're panicking from fright.

Pull out your list of passions again and take a long look at it. When you did your wheel of life exercise, which passion did you determine to be the most out of balance in your life? Is this where you would like to start? Would you like to bring that area more into alignment with your spirit, more into balance with the rest of your life? If yes, let's go for it! If no, then put that one on hold for now and choose another area of your life that you'd like to work on. Now, picture in your mind what a ten out of ten would feel like in this area of your life. Take a moment to close your eyes and really think about it. What would having this item balanced in your life feel like, look like, sound like? That is your ultimate goal.

For now, don't worry about how you will get there or how you will achieve it. We will cover all of that later in the book. Your vision may even seem impossible to you, but for now, trust me and write this down as your goal. Maslow said that in any given moment we have two options: to step forward into growth or to step back into safety. Make the leap of faith and vote for growth.

Earlier, I shared with you the story of philosopher, Brian Johnson. He stated that when he left law school for good and made the decision to follow his bliss, for him it was like stepping off a cliff, not knowing if there would be anything there to catch him. One of the scariest things he's ever done in his life. But he chose to trust and made the big leap and he's blissfully never looked back since.

Speaking of leaps, while you're thinking about your goals, tape a piece of blank flipchart paper high up on the wall. Mark on the paper with a pen the highest point that you can stretch to. Now see if you can stretch even further. Try and beat the mark you had put on the paper. Were you able to do it? Amazing what we can do if we only stretch ourselves a bit. If we push ourselves, and have faith in our ability, we can always do more.

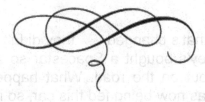

When devising your goals, you'll want to know that there are two types of goals: those which I call 'forward' goals (or those goals which take you in a forward direction, obviously) and 'away' goals (those which unwittingly take us further away from our target).

The fascinating thing about your subconscious mind is that it is like a heat-seeking missile and once you clearly define the target (your big goal), it will stop at nothing to achieve that target.

Film Director, Tracy Trost, describes it this way, "Your subconscious is working all the time, 24/7, and it's working at what you give it and it's going to bring about what you give it during your lifetime."

He had an interesting way of illustrating this when he asked me one day what type of car I drove.

"A Mitsubishi," I replied.

"What model?" he asked.

"A Spacestar."

"Okay, so when you bought that car, did you start to see more cars like that around?"

"It's not very common," I replied, "but yeah, I definitely did!"

"You noticed them, where you didn't notice them before."

"Exactly."

"The only thing that's changed . . . they didn't all of a sudden say, 'Hey! Shelley's bought a Spacestar so we need to put more of these out on the road. What happened was your subconscious was now being fed this car, so it looked for the car everywhere else. What you feed your subconscious is what it's going to notice, what it's going to lean toward."

So, the point is, you need to be very careful which type of target you clearly define for it to heat-seek. Is it a forward goal? Or is it an away goal?

What do I mean? A forward goal has a positive focus and takes you forward, closer to your target. An example might be, "I am going to vacation in Paris next May" or "I want to have another child before I am 30." In both cases, you have given your subconscious mind a clear specific target to aim its heat seeking missile at. You've instructed yourself, "Subconscious mind, I want you to find a way to have another child before I attain the age of thirty years." Your subconscious mind will reply, "Righty-ho! Done deal! You can put it in the bank!" And it will go get it for you if you do not block it.

"Subconscious mind, I want you to find a way for me to vacation in Paris this May!"

"Okay boss. Will do!"

An away goal, on the other hand, takes you farther away from what you actually intend to achieve. How does that work? By telling your subconscious mind to aim at the exact opposite of what you really want.

You see, your subconscious mind is actually a fairly simple work-horse. It will punch well above its weight and it will definitely get the job done "come hell or high water," to quote a popular colloquialism. However, it does not (EVER!) stop to evaluate the instructions you've given it. It's like the best obedient worker you could ever ask for, one who works damn hard and never questions your authority or your instructions. It just does exactly what you tell it to do. And unfortunately, the subconscious mind's vocabulary is a bit limited. It doesn't understand negatives (or words that negate) and therefore just ignores them.

So if you give it an away goal as a target, that's exactly what it will get you. If you tell your subconscious mind that your goal is to not eat sweets from now on, your diligent and obedient worker didn't understand the word "not" and therefore ignored it, so it just heard you tell it, "eat sweets from now on!" And your subconscious replies, "Okay, boss! I'll go to work on that right now for you!" As a result, your poor willpower is sabotaged from the start and you haven't got a chance! Your subconscious, without you realizing it, is driving you further and further away from your intended destination.

Any ideas on how to change this 'away' goal into a 'forward' goal? Perhaps something like, "From this moment forward, I consume only healthy food" (as one example).

Let's look at some further examples and see what you think. Are they forward goals or away goals?

1. I will double my sales target.
2. I will lose weight.
3. I will pay off all my debt before my 35th birthday.
4. I will sign up for piano lessons.
5. I don't want to be in this low-paying job anymore.

Well, what do you think? How about number one, I will double my sales target? Are we telling our heat seeking missile to hit a bulls-eye or to veer off into outer space? I presume we would know what our normal sales target is (say, for example $50,000), so then telling our subconscious specifically, "I want you to double your sales target!" would give it something fairly specific to aim at. It would know that 2 x $50,000 = $100,000 and would surge forward, answering, "Yes, boss!" The only caveat with this goal is that while the target is clear, the time frame is not. We've not actually told our subconscious mind when we expect it to go get this for us and as a result, it might be confused or think that mañana will be just fine. To alleviate this confusion, you can rewrite the goal with a specific time frame attached: I will double my sales target before the end of the month. Now that's a powerful goal!

So how about goal number two? Forward or away? What are you telling your subconscious specifically to go out and do for you, bearing in mind its few simple limitations? "Lose weight," you say. However, the subconscious can so easily get tripped up over this goal. "Lose" is a negative and an away action, leaving the subconscious to seek "weight" for you. Ouch! Additionally, we haven't even told our missile how much weight it's supposed to lose or when. Our goal is way too vague. Want to have a stab at rewriting this as a forward goal? Go for it! If it were my own goal, I would probably phrase it something like, "I will be five pounds slimmer by the 25th of June." Or, I will weigh 135 pounds by the 25th June. Your subconscious will reply, "I will? Oh! I guess I better get to work on that then!"

Goal number three: forward or away? Truthfully, it's probably fine as it is. However, because I am one who wants to be extremely clear about exactly what my goal is, therefore leaving absolutely no confusion for my subconscious mind, if it were my own goal, I would rewrite it to say something like, "I will achieve and maintain a totally positive cash flow by the first of next year." I've removed the word "debt" so that my subconscious can't get confused and focus on that as a target by mistake.

You see how removing any words that are things you don't want leaves your subconscious mind with only a positive, "forward" goal to take you to?

Goal number four. Is it a forward goal or an away goal? Hmmmm. Seems pretty clear to me. The target is piano lessons. You've told your subconscious to go sign up. It'll be immediately ready to jump into action . . . . except for one thing. We kind of forgot to tell our subconscious when we wanted it to go hit this target. We might mean immediately. Or we might mean next year as a birthday present to ourselves. Or we could mean after we retire and have a bit more time on our hands. To repair this confusion, just put a simple date on it and our subconscious will know exactly what it is supposed to do and when. "Sign up for piano lessons this weekend."

"Okay, boss!" your subconscious mind replies.

And finally, goal number five, our last example. I'm sure by now you're too clever to fall for my ruse. This is a classic example of an away goal, wherein you have instructed your subconscious to stay in a low-paying job and it will be very compliant and hard at work to get you exactly what you've told it you want. Have a go at rewriting this one yourself as a forward goal. Remember to make it crystal clear, something very specific to aim at (hint: like an exact salary figure), and remember to put a specific date on it.

In his article on SMART Objectives, Garry Platt, a senior consultant at Woodland Grange, said that your goal or action should be linked to a rate, number, percentage or frequency in order to be measurable. He uses answering the office telephone to illustrate this, saying "'Answer the telephone quickly' [as a goal] is not specific and allows for a subjective judgment to be made as to whether the outcome has been achieved. In contrast, 'answer the telephone within 3 rings' is specific."

Good on ya! I think you've mastered this segment quite well and are ready to explore in greater depth.

Brian Tracy advises, "The key to success is to focus our conscious mind on things we desire, not things we fear." The subconscious mind will then automatically follow. For example, if you are constantly worried about your bank account going into the red and that is what your conscious mind is constantly thinking about, you are unwittingly instructing your subconscious to follow suit. Remember what an obedient and hard little worker I told you it is? It will now begin to focus on your bank account and 'red ink' (debt), but remember it doesn't understand negatives and so just ignores them. So while your conscious mind is thinking, "Don't go in the red. Don't go in the red!" Your subconscious is being instructed to "Go in the red. Go in the red!" and guess what it will obediently do for you? It will, like a heat seeking missile, find ways to take your bank account into debt for you. Your car will mysteriously break down and require $400.00 worth of parts, while your child will tell you she needs $35 for a school field trip tomorrow that she forgot to tell you about. Aren't you proud of your obedient little puppy dog (the subconscious mind) for doing exactly what he's been instructed to do?

While science is in its infancy in exploring the limits of consciousness, many worthwhile studies have been done with regard to the subconscious mind. As far back as 1567, Paracelsus is credited with providing the first scientific mention of the subconscious (or unconscious mind, as he called it) in his work *Von den Krankheiten* (translated as "About Illnesses"), and his clinical methodology created an entire system that is regarded as the beginning of modern scientific psychology. Rather than cite hundreds of years worth of studies that have been performed and which have led to what we now know about the subconscious mind, I will leave you, if you're interested in such things, to research that on your own and I'll skip ahead to today's modern neuroscience and psychoanalytic theory supporting this concept.

In a recent study, researchers at Columbia University Medical Center found that fleeting images of fearful faces - images that appear and disappear so quickly that they escape conscious awareness - produce unconscious anxiety that can be detected in the brain with the latest neuroimaging machines. Your subconscious is active on a level that you are normally unaware of and it is consistently seeking evidence of your state of mind and your desires, so that it can bring you more of the same.

In the 1970s great advances in research were made. According to Wikipedia, the reach of these early findings was "significantly extended in the eighties and nineties by further research showing that outside of conscious awareness, individuals not only acquire information about frequencies (i.e., 'occurrences' of features or events) but also co-occurrences (i.e., correlations or, technically speaking, co-variations) between features or events. Extensive research on non-conscious acquisition of information about co-variations was conducted by Pawel Lewicki, followed by the research of D. L. Schachter (who is known for introducing the concept of implicit memory), L. R. Squire, and others."

Maxwell Maltz said that "when you refuse to turn your back on negative feelings, you put yourself in a position where it's like you're permitting termites to bore holes into your spiritual being, letting the fluids of your life force just flow down the drain." I love Maltz' metaphors because they are so vivid and right on point!

Scientists compare the mind to an iceberg. The 3-5% that you see "floating" above the water's surface is compared to our conscious mind. But then there is that hidden 95-97% that is so vast and unknown lying beneath the surface of the water and that 95-97% is likened to our subconscious mind in its potential.

Imagine that an iceberg decides it wants to take a little break and go on vacation. The 3% above the water's surface decides it might be nice to spend the winter in Florida for a change. However, the 97% beneath the water's surface has always wanted to see Alaska and is determined to vacation there. When push comes to shove and the bags are actually packed for leaving, who do you think will win? It's the hidden 97% . . . and so it is the same with our minds. The 97% of our brains known as the subconscious or unconscious mind wins every single time. So it is imperative to guard the thoughts you have and the instructions you are giving the subconscious, because there is no reasoning or argument with it.

Don't worry if it takes you a while to get this lesson in practical terms and fully integrate it into your life. Just keep trying until you master it. You will be all the better off for your perseverance in learning it and your evidence of mastery will be the consistent manifestation of that which you desire in your life.

As a final example in turning your thinking around, Bob Proctor offers this illustration:

> Jane earns a decent income - but she's not happy. She still has car payments, she wants to send her kids to a better school, she needs to save up for her graduate level education. But no matter how hard she works, she just never has enough. And to top it off - she owes the credit card companies tons of money.
>
> Odds are - you know someone like Jane.
>
> Most of us in Jane's situation will start to focus on what we DON'T have. But the problem is, when you fuss and complain about not having enough - you attract more bills to pay.
>
> Jane might set a goal to get out of debt. This, too, is the wrong approach . . . the goal of getting out of DEBT - keeps you forever in DEBT. You're thinking debt, debt, debt - and that's exactly what you attract into your life.
>
> This is how Jane would change her mindset . . .
>
> First she would change her goal. Her goal would no longer be "get out of debt." Her goal would be "absolute financial freedom." Now she's focusing on a positive. She would spend a few minutes every morning just day-dreaming about what she's going to do once she attains financial freedom.
>
> The next thing Jane would do is auto-correct her negative thoughts. Her initial thought might be:
>
> *I'm so badly in debt - I don't know what to do.*
>
> *I don't have enough to get the things I seek in life for myself and my family.*

Slowly, she'd start correcting these thoughts:

I shouldn't feel so bad - many people don't have a house or a loving family.

I have a home, my kids are happy. I have a loving family.

I have a nice job with an opportunity for a raise.

I am healthy.

My debt will be paid off - when I start saving just a little bit every month.

There are people far worse off than I - 1 billion people worldwide have to survive on less than a dollar a day.

I'm grateful that I have a job and a middle-income lifestyle.

I'm grateful that I have a car, nice clothes, can eat 3 meals a day, and can take the occasional vacation - most people cannot afford this.

I can believe that more money and multiple streams of income will open up to me in the near future.

I like the idea of being rich.

So, by gradually changing her view of her circumstances, Jane corrects herself from negative thinking to positive thinking [and opens new possibilities for herself].

I'll offer one final note about goals and the subconscious mind before we close this chapter. If you really want to ensure there is no delay or confusion on the part of the subconscious, especially with larger goals that will take some time to achieve, write them out as if you already have them in your life. Your subconscious then says, "Oh, we do?" It looks around for the evidence of it and, not seeing any (or enough of it), goes to work double-quick and even puts in overtime to provide evidence of what you already believe you have. "I weigh 135 pounds. I am flush with money and pay my bills in full the same day they arrive. I have a career that I love." Etcetera.

Take care, however, that you do not cancel out this positive action by immediately following it up with a negative thought that confuses your subconscious mind. For example, you state your goal as if you already have it, "I am flush with money and pay my bills in full the same day they arrive." Then you think, "No I don't. I'm always overdue paying my bills because I never have enough money to pay them on time."

In this example, you've just undone the instructions you intended to give your subconscious mind and you've reinforced your current set of instructions, reminding your subconscious that you wish to remain in debt and to have financial difficulties, despite your fleeting thought about financial flushness. Your subconscious, of course, will reply, "Yes, boss! I'll go get you that further indebtedness right now!"

If you find you are prone to this type of thinking ('correcting' your goals with 'reality') and you find it difficult to incorporate firm belief into your new set of goals, then you may wish to state them in such a manner as though you are in the process of getting them, rather than that you've already acquired them. It is difficult for your conscious mind to argue with that! Here is an example:

"I am creating multiple streams of income that will allow me to pay my bills in full on the day they arrive."

Here, you have told both your conscious mind and your subconscious mind that you are currently creating multiple income streams. Your subconscious mind will immediately set to work finding new income streams for you. Your conscious mind has a much more difficult time arguing with that statement, because for all it knows, you are. You are investigating new paths, seeking new opportunities, finding new ways to create additional income.

"I am so pleased that I am now being more careful about what I eat, so that I will be much healthier and slimmer."

Here, you have told both your conscious mind and your subconscious mind that you are currently being careful about what you eat. Your subconscious mind will immediately set to work paying attention to the nutritional qualities of the foods you choose and seek ways to bring healthier foods to you. Your conscious mind has a much more difficult time arguing with that statement, because for all it knows, you *are* beginning to eat more healthily. You are investigating new foods, seeking new opportunities to eat well, finding new ways to bring good, healthy foods into your diet.

Jack Canfield said, "I'm a big believer in growth. Life is not about achievement, it's about learning and growth, and developing qualities like compassion, patience, perseverance, love, and joy, and so forth. And so if that is the case, then I think our goals should include something which stretches us."

Which leads us right back to our original goal. Having decided which area of your life you wish to change, do you feel ready now to set a positive goal - one that you can unleash a heat seeking missile on? Then go on, set yourself a BIG, SCARY, FORWARD GOAL!!!! One that will cause you to have to stretch.

Maltz tells the story of his dear friend Salvador Dali who had painted a picture for him and "the picture was of the world. One half of the world was in shadow from frustration, where man's image had shrunken to the size of a small potato. The other half is in sunlight from confidence and there, man's image is ten feet tall and he's walking towards the sun." Which half of the world is your soul living in? Is it shrunken from living in the frustration of denying your true self and your passions, from just getting by day to day? Or is it living in sunlight and swelling with confidence, ten feet tall, touching the sun, and joyful from living a life of expressed passions and bliss? Banish frustration from your spirit. Set yourself some confident goals!

Once you've written a goal down you can subject it to the SMART test. SMART is an acronym:

Specific: Your goal should be specific and clear. Creating a specific and clear goal not only raises performance and achievement levels, but also determines the amount of effort required for success and provides a clear standard against which to measure progress. If you were a bomber pilot in World War II and I said your orders were to bomb the munitions factory in Germany, you'd say, "Yes, sir!" (just like your subconscious would say), but then you would scratch your head in confusion thinking, "Which munitions factory? Where in Germany?" I'd say, "Don't question your orders! Just do it!" How likely are you to succeed in your mission? You'd flounder around, flying back and forth over the entire country of Germany, wasting time, money and valuable resources looking for something that looks like a munitions factory . . . . only to discover you dropped your bomb on a primary school instead. So make sure any goals that you set are clear and specific. Leave no doubt as to exactly what the positive target is.

Measurable: You must be able to measure the extent to which your goal has been set, else how will you know when your goal has been achieved? To say, I want more money is insufficient, since "more" is not measurable. If you say, however, "My goal is to have one million dollars in my bank account on the 15th July 2015," for example, that is something that can be measured.

Achievable: Does your goal place you smack-dab in the middle of the stretch zone? Then you can rest assured it is achievable! Remember, your stretch zone will require you to employ a combination of your current skills and abilities together with the new ones you'll need to learn in order to achieve it. But it is not so far outside of your current skill set that it causes you to panic.

Relevant: Is your goal relevant to you? We discussed goals that are imposed from the outside and goals you would not normally adopt for yourself. These are a classic example of goals that are not relevant to you. At the other end of the scale, we also talked about your passions. These are not only relevant to you, they are vital in order for you to thrive! As long as your goals are relevant to you, goals which you perceive to be important to you and that match with your values, you will have a much greater chance of achieving them.

Time-Bound: We've already talked about how easily confused the subconscious becomes when there is no timeframe attached to a goal. You will need to place a time scale or a deadline on each of your goals in order to be successful at achieving them.

Brian Tracy said, "People with clear, written goals, accomplish far more in a shorter period of time than people without them could ever imagine." And he is correct. Scientific studies back this up.

Actress Halle Berry said, "The wisdom my mother taught me . . . is to run the race of life always looking forward and never behind. It's very hard not to look back, but I know she's right." So look forward and set yourself some forward goals right now.

I am inspired by the story of Jeanette McVoy, entrepreneur, executive at SOC and President at Profitable Marketing Systems.

She is also a former Registered Nurse at Jewish National Medical and Research Center. She set herself two goals: one to spend more time with her grandchildren and the other to become self-employed. She achieved both in a remarkable way.

Jeanette says, "I am a 63 year old former nurse who spent 39 years in nursing before starting my own home business. I had no business training of any kind and could never have done it without the personal help I got from my mentors.

Now, I make more than twice what I ever did as a Registered Nurse and work only 3 days each week so I can spend the other 2 days with my grandchildren.

I go to yoga whenever I want and get massages whenever I want. A few short years ago, I had to get up early just to make it to my job and then also had to work weekends at another job just to make ends meet.

My husband works the business with me on a part time basis and together we have risen to be number 19 out of 93,012 distributors in our company. One of the things we like about it so well is that we benefit personally and financially by helping others to achieve their goals.

How cool is that! We work when we want, with whom we want and get paid to help others to do the same.

In my blog called 12 Steps to Your Dream Life, which can be found at http://thecardwoman.com, I share what we have learned that has made us successful so that you can do it too - in whatever business is best for you.

What's important is the basic principles, not the specific business itself. The business that is best for you may be, and probably is, completely different than what works for me and that's just fine. I'll show you how to find it."

Jeanette definitely says, "You can do it, too!"

Chapter Three - Develop a Plan of Action

*"The key is not to prioritize
what's on your schedule,
but to schedule your priorities."*

Stephen R Covey

Well, thought is one thing and action is another.

Now that you've got a specific goal in mind . . . AND IT IS WRITTEN DOWN . . . it's time to formulate a rough map of how we're going to get to our destination. By defining both our goal and our plan of action, we can create a detailed picture of what we want to achieve and how we are going to achieve it.

Some people, though, get so bogged down in the planning of something and making sure that every little detail is accounted for that they never actually get around to doing that thing which they set about planning. It's a disease I call 'detail-itis' and it can sideline you just as quickly as any other serious disease.

So can procrastination.

But after a full day at work, you're tired and you just don't have the energy to start. So you have dinner, watch TV, fall asleep on the sofa and think: *"I'll do it tomorrow"*. But tomorrow never comes.

So how can you avoid these obvious traps? By making it easy to take immediate action! Action kills both procrastination and detail-itis dead.

I want you to look at your goals and see where you can break them down into even smaller steps, each of which contributes toward achieving your overall goal. You may end up with tasks that will take just 5-15 minutes to complete. Then select one of these small tasks and write it down on your to-do list for tomorrow. Achieving big, scary goals is as simple as taking the next baby step toward it.

After you've completed that 5-15 minute task, write down the next one to be achieved. Each day you'll complete a small task that is part of a larger goal and write down the next task for completion the following day.

For example, if your goal is to be fit and healthy, one of your objectives might be to reach your target weight by completing a 'work out' every day for 30 minutes.

If you are finding it difficult to get started, perhaps procrastinating, then break your larger goal into a mini-task (or baby step) such as:

"Do one exercise for lower abs, 5 times."

It could take you about 2-3 minutes to accomplish this. And you are much more likely to achieve it when you've put it at the top of today's to-do list with a high priority.

However, the sneaky thing about this approach is that you are likely to go on and complete the whole 30-minute routine, or at least maybe fifteen minutes, since the most difficult part is getting started. Once you get started, you will find out that you don't mind doing more than you planned. However, even if all you did was the "lower abs, 5 times," you would still be closer to your goal than if you hadn't done them . . . and you'll have surmounted the procrastination barrier. All you have to do is just add another baby step toward your goal to tomorrow's to-do list . . . perhaps 5 push-ups.

This approach offers the added bonus of helping you to avoid feeling guilty or depressed about not doing what you said you would do.

The same holds true for "detail-itis" - getting bogged down in the minutia of planning every little detail, such that we never actually get around to doing the thing we are planning. This is a common thing for perfectionists to do and indicates that the fear of making a mistake is greater than the desire to achieve the goal. Alfred Adler said, "Do not be afraid of *making mistakes*, for there is no other way of learning how to live!" John Bradshaw agreed. He said, "It's okay to make mistakes. Mistakes are our teachers - they help us to learn."

By holding onto your need for perfection, you are preventing yourself from achieving success in your life - success in whatever area of your life you have passions and goals for. Is that really what you want? Learn to let go.

We'll further discuss how to overcome this and other barriers to success later in the book. But for now, open your mind to thinking about just diving in and doing and learning along the way.

When traveling on this journey we call life, it is best to remain quite flexible and open to our instincts and intuition. To refer back to our vacation example from chapter one, if we were driving along and we could see the traffic building up and beginning to get quite heavy, we might decide it would be best to change course and take an alternate route (a lesser road), rather than remain on the clogged freeway, sitting motionless for hours. Or we may decide that allowing ourselves to be diverted would take us too far off course in the quest toward our goal and that the prudent thing to do is to be patient and have faith that a path will open up for us soon enough.

Either way, we need to pay attention to what our intuition is telling us is the NEXT STEP along our journey. Don't get bogged down with all the details of how the entire journey is going to come together. Just focus on and take the next step and watch the momentum build!

There is a Chinese Proverb that says, "Be not afraid of going slowly, but only afraid of standing still." There is much wisdom in this saying. Truthfully it makes no difference how long it takes us to achieve our goal . . . only that we keep putting one foot in front of the other, taking the next step in a forward direction, one foot in front of the other, baby step after baby step. And by doing this we are assured with a certainty that we WILL reach our destination, just as it is a forgone conclusion that if we start off in Los Angeles and drive along a specific route north, we will end up in Seattle. We cannot fail.

The key, obviously, is to maintain focus along the route so as not to be diverted off to New Mexico, along the way. However, as long as we maintain our focus and keep taking our baby steps forward, victory is assured.

This is where our action plan will help.

So now I want you to think of that big, scary goal you set for yourself in the last chapter - the one where I said, don't worry about how you're going to get there, we'll deal with that later. Well, later is now. At the top of a clean sheet of paper, write out this goal and label it your long-range goal. This is the big one that may take you three to five years to achieve. It's not just overnight.

I'm going to offer an example of "start my own business within three years" so that you can follow the process here, but I'd like you to stick to your own goals and apply the process to them in order to receive maximum benefit.

So there's my big, scary, long-range goal at the top of the page and at this point it would be really easy to throw my hands up in the air and say, "Oh my God! How am I ever going to achieve that!? It's not possible!" and then walk away. But stay with me, because I'm going to show you how it is not only possible, it is inevitable when you take baby steps.

In order to achieve this big, scary, long-range goal, I am going to need to break it up into medium and short range goals and then steps to achieve each. So I'll ask myself, "What needs to happen in order for me to start my own business?" Ask yourself the same question regarding your big scary goal. What needs to happen in order for you to achieve it?

Well, one of the things I will need to do is to quit my job, but that's definitely not the first thing I want to do! It just happens to be where my mind jumps to first. So on another sheet of paper I'm going to start a list.

1. Quit job.
2. Save/acquire enough money to quit job and start business. Maybe obtain financial backing.
3. Figure out what type of business I wish to start.
4. Locate the ideal premises,
5. Hire people, if needed. etc

You can see how the thought process begins. Write down anything and everything that comes into your head at this point. If you enjoy mind mapping, this is a great time to do it. We'll sort out the list into some semblance of order soon, but for now just list or mind-map everything you think of. It is easy at this point to become overwhelmed by the magnitude of the goal and the process required to achieve it. If you find that is the case in your situation, don't allow yourself to become paralyzed with fear. Draw back and focus on baby steps. Forget the whole process for now and ask yourself, simply, "What is the next step I need to take?" For my example, I think probably I would need to figure out what type of business it is that I wanted to do.

So the next question is, of course, "Okay, what do I need to do in order to do that?" Well, I would need to maybe look around at various types of businesses, maybe re-examine my passions and see if I could incorporate one or two of those, maybe do a bit of research. Okay . . . that's not so scary. I can do that.

If I focus only on my next baby step, then it is much easier for me to take action. I now start thinking about my passions, for example, and knowing that I love both travel and writing, I begin to think, "Hmmmmm, I wonder what it takes to become a travel journalist?" Your passion may be art and you might be thinking of possibly opening a shop that sells works of art and crafts. Or perhaps you combine your passion for art with a passion for travel and decide to think about leading tours through India for those that are into the fiber arts.

Either way, one baby step leads inevitably to the next. For my travel journalist goal, I now start doing a bit of research on the internet and I learn that while I could write a travel guide (i.e. a long book), certain magazines are happy to purchase articles on various locations, from freelance writers.

This opens up new possibilities for me. I can see possible options now that I couldn't see before. I'm actually a little excited because I might be able to see a way to obtain my big-scary goal. But hold on . . . that's really frightening me, so let's just focus on our next baby step. Right, what's our next baby step again? Oh yeah, maybe I should buy some of these travel magazines and see what their articles are like. Then I'll know what kind of articles they are wanting and what the overall flavor of the magazine is. Then after I've read the travel magazines, I'll contact the magazine editors and ask if they are looking to buy articles and how much they pay or maybe I'll find this information on their websites. Hey, I just remembered my friend, Sue, was saying that her sister-in-law works at Conde Nast! Maybe she can help me with a foot in the door or some information! I'll contact Sue and ask. In any event, once I have the information I need, then I can think about my next baby step.

I start planning my next vacation with a view to writing all about it and selling the article. I'll have an idea of what the magazine wants from me (Is it the planning process they want me to write about? The sights to see? Budget places to eat and stay?). I can begin to see how being able to write occasional articles in my spare time would allow me to continue working at my job, but explore whether it is viable for me to become a travel writer full time.

By having an end goal in mind, but not focusing on the entire process, by simply shifting my focus to only the next baby step, the path lays itself out before me and new possibilities open up that I can take advantage of. People and opportunities will present themselves that I might not even have thought about previously, because now I am able to remain flexible instead of being locked into an entire program or pathway. Since I am only focused on my current baby step, the next step I take after that can be in any direction I choose and usually suggests itself.

If this approach works for you, I want you to write out on a sheet of paper in VERY BIG letters this question, "What can I do today that will bring me one step closer to my goal?" Now put that sheet of paper in the most prominent place you can think of so that you have to see it several times a day. Get into the habit of asking yourself every day, "What is my next baby step?" and then following through by taking action on just that one baby step. In this way, you cannot fail to eventually reach your end goal.

However, if you are the type of person that likes to have the entire route planned out before you set off on vacation and that is your preferred method here (perfectionists often fall into this category), pull out that list you just made and let's take a look at it. You have your big, scary, long-range goal and you now have a list of shorter range goals and interim steps that you need to take in order to reach those. Your map will look somewhat like this:

Long-Range Goal = become self-employed within 3 years (travel journalist?)

Mid-Range Goal (within a year and half) = Sell enough articles each month to equal half my monthly salary at my job or write enough travel books (hard copies, e-books, audiobooks?) to equal one-half my annual salary at my job.

Short-Range Goal (within six months) - Have written at least two articles or three book chapters.

Now - Research all of the above and speak to a publisher or literary agent to find out about the travel book market. Purchase several travel magazines and contact their editors for more information.

Another example is the following:

Long-Range Goal = Retire to France within the next 36 months.

Mid-Range Goal (within 18 months) = Obtain French lawyer and real estate agent. Buy a 3-bedroom house in Brittany with a large garden, within 50 miles of Brest airport, within a price range of €250,000 to €300,000.

Short Range Goals (within 3-6 months) = Get finances in order. Choose local real estate agent. Prepare house for sale by putting unnecessary items into storage or selling them and obtain valuation of house. Research property market in Brittany and draw up list of real estate agents. Arrange tour of Brittany over the summer holidays. Choose which area I wish to live in.

Depending how detailed you like to be, you can now fill in all of the steps necessary to achieve your short-range, mid-range, and long-range goals. You can also ask yourself what possible barriers to success might lurk along the way and how you plan to overcome those. Are there certain people whose help you need to enlist in order to achieve your goal? What resources do you need in order to achieve each of the steps in your action plan?

By dividing up your long range goal into smaller, more immediate goals and even smaller interim tasks or steps, you avoid the trap of overwhelming yourself and not knowing where to start.

The trick though, as I said before, is to not get so bogged down in the details that you never take action. Don't allow yourself to get locked into a particular program or pathway, such that you are unable to remain flexible enough to respond when the universe presents you with opportunities you hadn't seen or even imagined before. When you become rigid and focused on how you are going to get where you are going, you are putting blinders over your eyes to your own detriment. Keep your mind on the end goal, but keep your focus on the next baby step you need to take and forget all the rest.

To resurrect the analogy of our summer vacation (again), if we are certain that the way we are going to get to Seattle from Los Angeles is along Interstate 5 and we remain closed to other options, we may find ourselves in trouble when we get to Medford and discover that there has been some mishap that has caused the closure of I-5 for the next week. Because we were closed to any other possibility, we ignored the signs along the way suggesting we take a diversion along the Coast Highway. We snapped at our partner when (s)he suggested we might want to do things differently. And we thought the local at the last gas station who offered to lead us to the Coast Road was a bit loony. We focused solely on the route we knew to be 'right', ignoring all other possibilities and to our detriment, we landed in Medford, stuck for a week or more, unable to go forward.

Bruce Lee said, "Empty your mind, be formless, shapeless - like water. Now you put water into a cup, it becomes the cup, you put water into a bottle, it becomes the bottle, you put it in a teapot, it becomes the teapot. Now water can flow or it can crash. Be water, my friend." Business mogul Andrea Jung agreed when she said, "Flexibility is one of the key ingredients to being successful. If you feel like it's difficult to change, you will probably have a harder time succeeding."

I am inspired by the story of Glenn Fisher, the editor at The Shortcut Bulletin, Agora Publishing in London. He says:

It strikes you . . . Writing a report on the allocation of European grant funding in North East Lincolnshire Council you suddenly realize that's not what you should be doing.

You carry on, though. That's what people do. They carry on.

But a week later, you're reconciling the contents of the various safes in the parks and open spaces of the region.

You're counting cash. Hmmm. You realize again, this isn't what you should be doing.

But you carry on. That's what people do. They carry on.

Finally, you're taking a random sample of student loan payments and checking the right amount has been paid. But you carry . . .

No. Something clicks. You stop.

That nagging feeling - that this is not what you should be doing - becomes not so much a feeling as a huge repeating slap about the face.

You take action . . .

Everyone's had some job they didn't like. You might even be in one now.

You dream of a change but the salary - not its size, but its security - holds you back.

You might have little Timmy and Tanya who get home from school and need feeding . . .

You might have that loved one who you want to be able to treat as often as possible . . .

You might have those parents who need looking after now they're not so mobile . . .

You can't afford to just quit it all.

It's unrealistic.

The key is to start small.
I didn't just quit the local council in a flash.

When that nagging feeling finally started slapping me in the face, what I actually did was make a small but fundamental decision . . .

To take action.

I carried on working . . .

I had to do an audit of the loans and investments department which nearly bored me to death, I had to carry on going into local schools to analyze the financial systems they had in place, I had to carry on counting other people's money.

But I started doing something else . . .

One evening a week I attended a writing class at the local college. You see, I knew I wanted to write in some way and make money from my writing. But you can't just become a professional writer overnight . . .

And it's the same for developing a second income stream that you love doing: it doesn't just happened overnight.

So, you take one small step. At just two hours a week, the writing class was that step.

From there, it begins to spiral.

I realized I could take it a step further and study writing on a more permanent basis. From there I discovered copywriting and information publishing and from there . . .

Well, here we are. I'm now the Editor of The Shortcut Bulletin, doing work that I love.

Don't get me wrong. From that small but fundamental decision to take action I've had a good run.

But the key here, what I want you to take away from this, is that I only got to where I am because I made that decision, because I started small and set the ball rolling.

It's this very same mentality that is so important to your own success.

What you need to do - if you haven't already - is to make that decision . . . that decision to take action.

Whatever it is you want to do, just keep in mind that you do not need to do it overnight.

Your success will come, but you must be patient.

You must start by taking a small step and only from there will you be able to escalate your efforts and eventually, as I say, your success will come.

Best wishes,

Glenn Fisher

Obviously, Glenn's message here is that "You can do it too!"

Chapter Four - The Power of Focus

*"There are only two words that will always lead
you to success. Those words are yes and no.
Undoubtedly, you've mastered saying yes. So
start practicing saying no. Your goals depend
on it!"*

Jack Canfield

In this fast-paced and busy world, it is very easy to wind up with 'too much on our plate', so to speak. We have days (or weeks, months, years, lifetimes) where we have to rush around in the morning, get breakfast on the table, get the kids off to school, get our partner out the door, and then be off to work ourselves. We have deadlines to meet, projects to complete, people to see, and targets to achieve. We get home from work and we have to put dinner on the table, wash the dishes, throw some laundry in the washing machine, bathe the kids and read them a story, put them to bed, throw the clothes in the dryer, lay out the kids' clothes for tomorrow and our own, pack lunches, and take a shower before flopping into bed, exhausted, so that we can get up the next morning and do it all over again.

With all of that going on in our lives, it is very easy sometimes to lose focus of our larger dreams and goals. This is why you have a greater chance of success if your goals are set from a starting point of passion and why it is very important to write them down. Your motivation to stay focused will be much higher. And working toward and achieving your goals will actually energize you when they come from a point of personal passion.

Let's say your passion was a love of music and that you had set yourself a goal of learning to play the piano. Taking an hour and a half each week (including travel time) to learn something new that you are passionate about enthuses you and seems like no time at all. No sooner have you arrived than it's time to go. You set aside a half hour a day to practice and because you are so excited about your music, the half hour flies by! You wish you had more time! Additionally you feel energized by having set aside some 'me-time' in which you were able to just focus on something you yourself love. You begin having creative ideas about your music and this energizes you even more.

"Yes, but where on earth am I going to get an extra half hour a day," you wail.

Jack Canfield, through his own years of experience in this area, offers some sound advice. He says, "Success depends on getting good at saying no without feeling guilty. You cannot get ahead with your own goals if you are always saying yes to someone else's projects. You can only get ahead with your desired lifestyle if you are focused on the things that will produce that lifestyle." Can you rearrange your life by saying no to (or delegating to someone else) some of the things that take time away from what you really want?

For example, perhaps you can take turns with a neighbor driving the kids to school. She can drive your kids two days a week and you can drive hers two days a week. You've just bought yourself an extra hour a week. Maybe your sister might be willing to watch the kids for you on Saturday afternoons if you'll watch hers on Sunday afternoons. If so, you've just bought yourself another three hours. Do you really need to show up at every PTA meeting and act as president of the local clean-up-the-park committee? Can you be involved in a lesser way? If so, you've just gained more time to devote to your passions. Go back to chapter one and look at your Wheel of Life again. What are those areas of your life that are time and energy drains, the things that you can let go of and be all the better off for it?

Steven Covey said, "It's easy to say 'no!' when there's a deeper 'yes!' burning inside."

Actress Debra Messing said. "Learning how to say no is one of the most exciting, liberating things I've learned to do in my whole life." She has a point. When we let go of those things in our life that are draining us of our time and our energy, it is like we are letting go of a ball and chain hanging around our necks. We open ourselves up to a multitude of possibilities - possibilities that we can say 'yes!' to because we've learned to say 'no!' to time and energy drains.

We can begin to create focus on our dreams and goals.

Close your eyes for a moment and picture in your mind exactly what your end goal is . . . that thing you wrote down in chapters two and three . . . . that big, scary, long-range thing that you would love to have in your life if only it were possible. Picture yourself actually having achieved it. How does that feel? What does it look like? Close your eyes and think about that for a few minutes.

This visualization exercise will become a vital part of the journey toward your achievement of your dreams. If you keep the phrase *"You are what you think"* at the top of your mind, visualization will be of great use to you your whole life long. Repeat the phrase like a mantra until it becomes ingrained and part of your personal set of values. Because until that is the case, no real change will be possible for you!

Bob Proctor said, "We each possess in us remarkable reserves of power - just waiting to be tapped and properly channeled. And yet most of us lead quiet, ordinary lives. Imagine for a moment, if Superman used his powers to do nothing more than save kittens stuck in trees." Well, that is how your life is right now - a vast reserve of untapped power. Use your creative energy to really imagine what your life would be like if you were successfully to completely integrate your passions into your life and get rid of all time and energy drains. Close your eyes and just picture it for a few minutes. What would your life be like? Can you picture it?

When you are fully focused on your goals and are able to channel your thoughts as if you had already achieved your desires, you begin to expand your mind and unleash your full potential. In order to channel this focus, you need to be able to do this at will, not only daily, but several times a day. When you are driving to work, think about your goals. What will it mean to have achieved them? When you are sitting at your desk at work, think about how your life will have changed once your passions are fully integrated.

In chapter two, we talked about the power of the subconscious mind. The greatest gift you can give yourself (and your subconscious) is laser focus on your goal coupled with positive belief and certainty that you will attain it. This powerful combination creates an unstoppable force that has been seen many times throughout history.

In 1519, when Hernán Cortés landed his ships on the shores of the Yucatán Peninsula of Mexico, preparatory to invading, he envisioned for himself victory and wealth, even though the enemy outnumbered him by at least 4 to 1. Undaunted by the odds, Cortés wanted to instill in his men the same vision of victory, but he needed to make sure they really believed they could do it. In order to win, he needed to leave no room for doubt in their minds. He had the men unload their supplies from the ships after landing and then ordered every one of the ships burned. His men were aghast. Why would he do such a thing? For Cortés it was all or nothing. He told his men that the only way for them to go back home to Spain was to win the impending battle and to return in enemy ships. The sheer fact that he was willing to die in this endeavor showed his resolve.

Cortés' men conquered the Aztecs and succeeded where others had been unsuccessful for six centuries previous.

There is a powerful lesson here. One of the keys to reaching your own goals is to eliminate any escape routes. It is tempting to retreat to the safety of your comfort zone when challenges and difficulties arise. To avoid turning back and abandoning your goals, you must make going forward more compelling than going back and one of the ways to do that is to develop a powerful vision with heartfelt emotion and true belief behind it.

Bob Proctor said, "Whatever you think about, whether it's good or bad - you attract into your life. Whether you want it or not is irrelevant - think about something you DON'T WANT and you attract it into your life. Worry about getting out of debt - and that's what you attract - MORE debt. Worry about getting old - and you'll start experiencing the effects of old age. Worry about whether or not he or she loves you - and you attract uncertainty into your relationships." So it is important to learn to create a laser-like focus on what you WANT to bring into your life.

One of the challenges that presents itself when we think about maintaining focus is distraction. The mind cannot hold two thoughts at once. Napoleon Hill said that, "Positive and negative emotions cannot occupy your mind at the same time." It is the same with goal-oriented thoughts. Our mind cannot go in two directions at the same time. Therefore, when we allow ourselves to focus on a distraction, our attention is divided and we lose focus on our goals.

Zajonc, Cottrell, Schmitt, and many other social psychologists have done studies over the last 45 years on the effects other people have with regard to our focus on goals. It has been found that the results will depend on the group dynamic, but you will achieve one of two results: either social loafing or social facilitation. In other words, one group of people can cause you to be dragged down and slacken (loaf, in essence) when it comes to focus on your goal. Another group can facilitate the achievement of a goal and, essentially, spur you on or drive you towards it.

Since this is a key element to successful achievement of your dreams, what kind of people do you surround yourself with? Do they help you focus on your goals? Or do they distract you away from them? Start thinking about surrounding yourself with people that assist you in focus on your goals and minimizing association with those who distract your focus and cause you to slacken off your progress toward your goals.

No man is an island and no one can achieve success in reaching their goals without the help and cooperation of others.

Don't even think of 'going it alone'. Surround yourself with the right group of people, those that will assist you in achieving your goals. By doing this, you create synergy. Thomas D. Willhite said, "When a human being has synergism, a mysterious third force enters their life . . . one plus one equals three not two. The whole becomes greater than the sum of its parts." It's a fascinating scientific phenomenon.

Hill said that a group of minds coordinated in a spirit of harmony will provide more thought energy than a single mind, just as a group of electric batteries will provide more energy than a single battery. Enthusiasm is contagious and teamwork is the inevitable result. For example, the best football team relies more on harmonious coordination of effort than individual skill to achieve a win. The greatest successes in life come to those who work harmoniously with others. When your personal goals coincide with those of another, not only does the power of your combined labors benefit you, but such cooperation also creates a synergistic effect that allows you to achieve far more than the simple sum of your individual efforts.

Build yourself a team that'll get in the scrum with you, as well as a good group of cheerleaders that will spur you on.

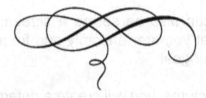

Returning to the concept of visualization, one of the best ways to develop focus is to create for yourself what's called a 'vision board'. Take a bulletin board or a sheet of cardboard, or even the front of your refrigerator . . . it really doesn't matter, as long as it is a flat surface that's large enough. Now go through magazines, trawl the internet, and seek pictures that represent your goals to you. If your goal is to bring a man into your life, cut out pictures of the type of man you desire. Is he tall? Short? Funny? Intelligent? Be specific with your words and pictures. Get as much detail into them as you can. Is it a new home that you want? What type? Where in the world? On the water? In a forest of trees? On acreage? Does it have two floors? More? Less? How many bedrooms and bathrooms? Again, be as specific as possible.

Paste as many pictures that represent your goals as you can to your vision board and then place your vision board in a prominent place where you have to look at it, not only every day, but preferably several times a day.

Hill said, "Keep your mind ON the things you want and OFF the things you don't want!" A vision board is a great way to do that.

Another alternative is the 'mind movie'. This is a short (2-5 minutes) film that you can create (or have created for you) with upbeat music and pictures (still or moving) of those things that represent your goals. Place the movie on your computer's desktop or on your iPod and watch it a couple of times a day, especially once before you go to sleep at night.

A mind movie can also be set as a screen saver on your computer, so that you are randomly and frequently exposed to pictures of your goal.

By using vivid pictures, you will create a determined focus for your subconscious mind and it will develop the drive to take you to your goal's achievement.

Another very powerful method of bringing focus to bear on your goal is to take up meditation. Don't say you don't have the time, because it can be done in as little as ten minutes a day, yet for such a small investment it can yield dynamic and compelling results.

Throughout the day, our minds are in constant movement, generating an incessant flow of thoughts that either make us feel happy or bring us pain. These uncontrolled fluctuations have the ability to create a clutter of inner anxiety that keeps us in a state of stress and disables positive thoughts. Learning to calm your mind will enable you to develop the inner tranquility that is indispensable in visualizing the achievement of your goal.

So, the purpose of meditation is to learn to cut out the constant 'noise' and 'chatter' that runs through your head and to empty the mind, bringing your attention and focus to only one thing . . . your breath, for example. When you are able to clear your mind of garbage, it is amazing the insight and the ideas that will come to you, as well as the clarity of thought and purpose. Try it!

Put the book down now and sit comfortably with your spine straight. Do not feel like you need to be some yogic pretzel in order to achieve harmony. It's not necessary. Perhaps a dining chair might work best for you. If so, place your feet flat on the ground and sit with your spine straight and in alignment, while the rest of you is totally relaxed. Close your eyes and focus on the sound of your breathing. Inhale deeply. Feel your chest rise and fall as you breathe. Feel your abdomen fill and then empty again as you breathe in and out. For the next ten minutes focus on nothing else except your breathing. If a thought enters your head, just gently dismiss it and bring your focus back to your breathing. See if you can go the entire ten minutes without thinking about anything except your breath.
This is an excellent discipline for creating focus and ignoring distractions. I highly recommend doing this once a day and as your discipline improves, increase your stamina by building the length of time you are able to focus. This little exercise also offers the added bonus of ridding your body and mind of stress and alleviating tension and worry.

Another way to create focus is to begin keeping a journal. I am NOT talking about the writings of a lovesick teenager, rehashing the angst of their daily dramas. What I am proposing is that you begin to write, on a daily basis, something positive about yourself, something you are grateful for, and something you did that day, however tiny or grand, that took you closer to your goal - whether it was making a phone call, doing 5 minutes of research, practicing a meditation, anything and everything . . . write it all down. You will be amazed at the effect this has on your subconscious mind in causing it to create for you more opportunities to take you closer to your goal.

There are only three rules in keeping your success journal:

1. Write only what you have done; *not* what you've still to do or what you are going to do tomorrow, or what you've failed to do. Write only what you have done toward your goals.
2. List even the small things. Everything counts! A phone call, a chapter read in a book, a decision to pass up a chocolate chip cookie. However small, it is an achievement on the way to your larger goal and small steps do add up, eventually taking you to your greater goal.
3. Make it a daily habit. Don't skip a single day even if you're tired. Just write a sentence or two.

Creating a daily journal will:

1. Motivate you - By writing down your achievements you will be able to see and feel real progress.

2. Eliminate distraction and temptation - It is easier to resist distractions and temptations if you know you are going to write down what you have accomplished towards your goal, every night!

3. Simplify - Things appear to be much simpler when you write them down. A journal helps you to create clarity in your life.

Remember in this journal that NO NEGATIVE is ALLOWED! You are not allowed to berate yourself for not having done something as well as you would have liked. You are not allowed to say that you didn't get around to doing today's baby step. ONLY POSITIVE COMMENTS ALLOWED in this journal, because we are working to create focus!

Additionally, if you know that every night before you go to bed, you have to sit down and take five minutes to write out what you did today that took you closer to your goal and then separately you also write your to-do list for tomorrow, including tomorrow's planned baby step, you are much more likely to get that thing done, whatever it is that was on your list for today, before you go to bed tonight. It's a method of creating accountability to yourself. By establishing self-discipline, you are creating the process that ties together all your efforts of controlling your mind, highlighting your personal initiative, utilizing positive mental attitude, and marshalling your enthusiasm.

Hill said that without self-discipline, you are as dangerous as a car running downhill without brakes or a steering wheel.

So, begin keeping a journal. You need not write long tomes - just a sentence or two a day will be a good start. Once you've gotten into the habit of writing every day, add in a few more sentences of positive things that will spur you on. Consider appreciating your own strengths and good qualities, as well as appreciating the assistance of others. Add in other things in your life that you are grateful for. Try this for thirty days and see what a difference it will make in your attitude and the achievement of your objectives. It is a powerful tool in creating focus.

And finally, if you are to ever achieve your goals, no matter what they are, there is a final exercise to master that will bring you positive focus on your goals like no other. For some, this exercise will be easy. For others it may prove the most difficult of all. But for everyone it will be necessary, and that is to shift your focus to that of an internal locus of control.

What do I mean? I'm talking about how you view yourself and how you view the world around you. Are you an optimist or a pessimist?

When something good happens, an optimist pats himself on the back, saying he did a good job. He has an internal locus of control. He believes that whatever happens is within his own realm of control and that he has responsibility for it.

What about the pessimist? He is more likely to attribute the success to luck, other people's hard work, or something else outside of his control. He has an external locus of control.

When something bad happens, the optimist looks to things outside of himself to explain the event - from bad luck to an off day - and he believes the event is only temporary, fleeting.

The pessimist, although he didn't take responsibility for the good event, is eager to take responsibility for the bad event, blaming himself and he tends to think that the negative is a more permanent situation.

What's worse is that the pessimist is more likely to make this self-blame and these external (occasional) bad events pervasive and universal. The pessimist thinks it is representative of his whole life. Whereas, the optimist tends to view a bad event as an isolated and temporary incident. A fluke. Nothing to get ruffled over, as life will get back on track any moment now, anyway.

With a good event, the pessimist will tend to isolate it, calling it a fluke or an accident, whereas the optimist is more likely to extend it to their whole life, believing that the positive event is representative of the greater good that is happening throughout their life.

So how about you? Where is your locus of control? Do you see yourself as a victim of circumstance? Or do you shift responsibility to yourself for the good that happens in your life, viewing the negative as just an occasional and temporary fluke?

Why would you want to be optimistic? After years of documented research, Seligman states that, "Life inflicts the same setbacks and tragedies on the optimist as on the pessimist, but the optimist weathers them better."

Bob Proctor offers an interesting perspective on shifting our thoughts by suggesting various circumstances that one might consider 'negative'. He explains how the optimist might view these situations and how you can shift your own focus:

> **Bed-Ridden in Hospital:** Decide that you're going to use this free time to learn something fun, say a new

language. Now you're thinking about a new skill rather than focusing on your illness.

Got Laid Off: Set a goal to find a job that pays you 25% more than your previous job. Think about this new job and stop thinking about being laid off. Start job hunting. Do not hold any negative feelings towards your boss for laying you off. Instead, think of him as having done you a favor because you're now going to find a better job.

Someone Owes You Money and Refuses to Pay Up: Forgive them. As long as you hold a grudge, you're telling the Universe that you've lost money. And indeed, you'll attract more loss. Instead, set a goal to earn twice the amount of money you've lost.

Got Dumped: Decide that you'll find a new love. Someone better suited to you. Make a list of all the qualities you'd love to see in your ideal mate. Now focus on meeting this new person.

Lost a Business Due to Bankruptcy: Decide that you're going to rebuild a new business and regain your financial freedom. Set a goal to earn 3 times what you previously had. Bonus Points: Decide that you're going to earn so much more that you'll be able to repay all your debts - even though you legally may not have to.

Groucho Marx said, "I, not events, have the power to make me happy or unhappy today. I can choose which it shall be."

How about you? Do you choose to be happy? It is a choice, you know. It's not just something that happens to you.

Karim Hajee tells the story of a gentleman he coaches. He says that the recent economic downturn threw him for a loop.

He got laid off . . . something he wasn't expecting and it happened just as he was preparing to get married. Michael remembered that he could call me whenever he had questions so he took me up on my offer.

He explained what had happened and how he was concerned that he wouldn't be able to find a job in such a tough market. Michael is a school teacher and had worked mainly in private schools.

He asked me what he should do and how he should apply what I'd taught him.

When Michael called me one of his first comments was:

"I'm worried about finding a job in this kind of market. Things are tough out there and I don't want to fool myself into thinking it's going to be easy."

My response: *"Don't be worried and don't be concerned. The job you want already exists, otherwise you wouldn't want it. You just have to find it. So let's focus on what you want, let's focus on attracting the opportunities and let's be open to all possibilities."*

The last part is always the toughest. Being open to all possibilities. Because this means being open to the possibility of doing something other than teaching in a private school or doing something completely different from teaching.

When you're open to all possibilities you trust that your higher self will guide you to what is best for you. What you want is still valid, but now you're open to something even better. The possibilities are endless.

We went over a number of things including the economy. Here's what I suggested:

Yes the economy is not great - but people are still hiring. There's always a need for teachers especially good teachers. Private schools suffer when the economy nosedives . . . but usually there are always jobs . . . regardless of the economy.

This belief has to be ingrained . . . you have to firmly believe that the job you want exists . . . it took a few sessions but Michael finally got it.

He called me back a few weeks later and said he finally understood that the job he wanted existed and that he would find it. But there was still that nagging doubt. He was concerned he wouldn't make the right impression, say the wrong thing, come across as nervous.

We had to get his [conscious] mind and subconscious mind to look at the positive side . . . that way he would attract positive situations and opportunities.

I explained that while he had accepted that this job existed, he didn't quite believe that he would get the job. I explained that he had to focus on his positive qualities and his strengths. Being nervous wasn't really an issue because as a teacher, he was used to speaking in front of people even in some trying situations.

He realized he had to look at things differently and focus on his positive qualities and strengths . . . so that his subconscious mind focused on the positive and not the negative.

We then created some specific affirmations, targeted to help him achieve his goal and create the belief he needed to succeed.

Michael went to work and applied the material regularly. That was roughly a month and a half ago.

Earlier this week I got an email from him and (not surprisingly) he got the job he wanted. Michael explained he had been on 3 interviews and got all 3 job offers.

Pretty cool huh? And it only took less than a couple of months.

He knows he's made the right choice.

Michael succeeded because he changed his beliefs. He didn't let his reality decide his future. He created his future by directing the power of his subconscious mind to create the success he wanted. He focused on his positive qualities. Michael believed in himself and his ability. He applied his learning and stuck with it.

You too can have the same success. Start creating the life you want. Start creating the success you want and deserve. Direct the power of your conscious and subconscious minds to help you succeed.

This concept of learning to shift your focus is vital to successful achievement of your goals. In considering your locus of control, think about how often during a typical day, you criticize, condemn, or complain. How can you, instead, shift your focus to the positive that might come out of that seemingly 'negative' situation?

Brian Johnson asks, "You get a parking ticket? Lose your job? Relationship not working? Kids being a challenge? Get sick?" It happens to all of us. He then says, "Of course, any and all of the challenges we face in our day to day lives can bring us turmoil, but NEVER forget that, ultimately, how *you* CHOOSE to respond to the challenge is entirely *your* call. DO NOT be a victim to the myriad of petty things that we can CHOOSE to let bother us. Own your attitude. CHOOSE how you will respond to any given situation. My personal recommendation?

Flip it around and think about all the things for which you're grateful.

Get a parking ticket? Be grateful you even have a car. Be grateful you're going to be able to help pay for someone's wages for part of the day. Stub your toe? Be grateful you HAVE a toe to stub and such a great life that that's probably the worst thing that's going to happen to you today. Kids being a little challenging? Be grateful they're healthy enough to make so much noise and honor them for the growth you both experience together. Whatever it is, choose your optimal response. Now."

While you're pondering this, T Harv Eker expanded the idea of conscious choice with reference to financial success, however what he says applies to all abundance in life; physical, spiritual, and mental. Notice the contrast between those with an 'abundance mentality' and those with a 'shortage mentality'. He said:

> Rich people believe "I create my life."
>
> Poor people believe "Life happens to me."
>
> If you want to create wealth [or anything else], it is imperative that you believe that you are at the steering wheel of your own life, *especially* your financial life. If you don't believe this, then you must inherently believe that you have little or no control over your life. Therefore, you have little or no control over your financial success. This is **NOT** a rich attitude.

Instead of taking responsibility for what is going on in their lives, poor people choose to **play the role of the victim**.

How can you tell when people are playing the victim? There are 3 obvious clues:

Victim Clue #1: They Blame

Victim Clue #2: They Justify

Victim Clue #3: They Complain

Have you ever noticed that there's no such thing as a really rich [or happy] victim? If you have chosen to seek wealth in life, it is imperative that you **choose your thoughts and words wisely**.

He then offers a challenging exercise. Are you up to it? He says, "Here's some homework that I promise will change your life. For the next seven days, I challenge you to not complain at all. Not just out loud, but in your head as well. But you have to do it for the full seven days. Why? Because for the first few days, you may still have some 'residual crap' coming to you from before. Unfortunately, crap doesn't travel at the speed of light, you know, it travels at the speed of crap, so it might take a while to clear out."

In Eker's own words, "When you are complaining, you become a living, breathing, crap magnet."

Can you do it? Try living the optimist's life for the next seven days. Work hard not to blame, criticize, condemn or complain. Instead, work to make people feel better about themselves for having been in your presence. Sincerely compliment them. Notice their strengths and comment on them.

Adopt the optimist's attitude and see the good in your own life as something to be proud of and grateful for and any bad that might occur as a temporary fluke, something that will quickly pass . . . or 'residual crap' as Eker puts it. If you catch yourself slipping back into your old ways, just correct yourself and try again. Be persistent and you will, in time, shift your thinking. Journal your successes.

Hillary Mantel said, "Arm yourself in advance against the setbacks every life contains. Scan your whole life and list 100 good things: compliments, achievements major and minor. It doesn't matter if they are things no one else would see as important; they are things that matter to you. If you meet an obstacle, sit down, take a breath, and read your list. Two things happen. Instantly, you feel better; and the problem, now set in the context of your whole life, seems smaller." Your journal is a great place to do that.

The much-revered Indian saint, Vivekananda, who lived over 100 years ago, explained it beautifully:

> All the powers in the universe are already ours. It is we who have put our hands before our eyes and cry that it is dark.

> We are what our thoughts have made us; so take care about what you think. Words are secondary. Thoughts live; they travel far.

> When an idea exclusively occupies the mind, it is transformed into an actual physical or mental state.

> We reap what we sow. We are the makers of our own fate. No one else has the blame; no one else has the praise.

I am inspired by the story of billionaire Bill Bartmann, a man whose story is so incredible, at times it defies belief.

Bill was raised in a family that worked hard, but knew nothing of wealth - his father was a janitor and his mother cleaned houses and raised the children. True to Bartmann family history and being from the wrong side of the tracks, Bill dropped out of high school and joined a gang.

Since the only way to survive in a gang is to get tough, Bill focussed his attention on being hard. At 16 years old and weighing only 98 pounds, he learned to set his first goal, perhaps purely from a survival instinct and he learned karate, boxing, judo, and wrestling to such levels of mastery (black belt, golden glove, etc.) that people thought he was intent on beating everyone up. "No" says Bill, "I was fixated on a target," (not getting beat up himself) and he achieved it. Yet there is where the story only begins.

Bill agrees with Nietzsche's philosophy, "That which does not destroy us, makes us stronger" and he subscribes to the idea that adversity introduces a person to him or herself. "That's when you find out who you really are and what you're really made of." Bill, of all people, should know, but not just because gang life taught him this.

Bill then decided to create a new challenge for himself and, although no Bartmann as far back as they could trace their family tree had *ever* graduated high school, Bill (the high school dropout) decided he wanted to go not just to college, but law school, no less.

Focussed on his goal, he managed to get into college on academic probation, where he further learned to focus his attention in order to achieve his goal of graduation. Several years of intense focus later, he says, "The day my parents came to Drake University in Des Moines to watch me be sworn in as an attorney and they could watch me walk across the stage and the Chief Justice of the Iowa Supreme Court handed me my sheepskin and I could walk back to the table and hand it to them . . . that was the one moment in their lives that they realized how important they were, because they had created an environment that allowed me to exceed them. And that's what every parent wants . . . The feeling it gave them was far more important than the feeling it gave me . . . They were euphoric."

Bill learned that he didn't have to come from the right side of the tracks, or be smarter than anyone else. All he had to do in order to achieve his goal was FOCUS!

"I learned from this college and law school era that I didn't have to be the smartest guy in the class. If I could just take all the noise and chatter and turn it off, if I could just see what's really important, just focus on what I needed to know and not listen to the distractions, it became an amazing outcome."

Once graduated, his next thought was to ask himself how well this newfound lesson applied to the business world. "When I graduated, I had one goal in my life and that was to become financially successful. So I became obsessed with what I had to do to become . . . filthy stinking rich." He set a goal to be listed in the Forbes 400 wealthiest people in America.

Choosing to focus all of his energy on his goal, he gave up all hobbies and outside activities and created a laser beam focus on attaining wealth. He achieved his goal and became the 25th wealthiest person in America, of course being listed in the Forbes 400. His company, CFS, was a 3.5 billion dollar international company.

"While that's a great story," comments Bill, "it's just one example of what you can do when you focus your energies." Not bad for a high school dropout from the wrong side of the tracks.

Bill is a firm believer that goals without focus are "just not gonna happen!" You can't achieve one without the other.

An interesting twist was added to his life story in 1998 when Bill's former business partner at CFS was indicted for fraud and sent the company into bankruptcy.

Although Bill's former business partner told the prosecutors that he had acted without Bill's knowledge, admitted his guilt and was sent to prison, the US Attorney General, John Ashcroft, in the post-Enron business environment, also felt compelled to indict Bill and, as a result, Bill lost everything material he had ever worked for.

Five years later, after a two month trial where the government called 53 witnesses and produced over 1,000 exhibits, Bill rested his case without calling a single witness or producing a single exhibit. The jury unanimously acquitted Bill on all counts.

Ironically, 17 months after his acquittal and six and a half years after his company was liquidated, the Federal Bankruptcy Trustee issued his report which publicly acknowledged for the first time, "CFS was not a fraud".

The good that came from this experience was that Bill learned his own core values.

Having attained all of his previous goals and seeing how well the power of focus works, Bill re-evaluated his life and determined that he didn't need to be a tough a guy, didn't need to be a smart guy, didn't even need to be a rich guy. What Bill wanted to set as his next goal was to be a happy guy. "Just to be happy. Happy with my wife, happy with my children, happy with my grandbabies, and now they are the most important thing in my life. They trump all else."

Needless to say, he has now achieved this goal, as well. "My focus now is my family. Oh yes, I make money. Oh yes, I give speeches. Oh yes, I write books. Oh yes, I'm on TV. Oh yes, all of that other stuff happens, but all of that other stuff is second to what my focus is, my family."

When making a life change, Bill asks himself two questions, "Am I doing what I think is right? Am I doing what I'm supposed to be doing [to achieve my goals]?"

Bill may be the only high school dropout who has:

- Been named "National Entrepreneur of the Year" (Twice) by USA Today, NASDAQ, Inc. Magazine, Ernst & Young, and The Kauffman Foundation

- Been inducted into the "Entrepreneur of the Year" Hall of Fame

- Created novel financial instruments that are still being used on Wall Street

- Had Harvard Business School use him as a case study

- Been granted a permanent place in the Smithsonian Institution's Museum of American History

- Been included in the Forbes Magazine list of the 400 Wealthiest Americans

- Named as "One of the Top 100 Entrepreneurs of the Last 100 Years" by the Kauffman Center for Entrepreneurial Leadership, Allbusiness.com, and Apple Computer

- Had his management techniques published in college text books and taught at universities across America

- Been awarded the American Academy of Achievement's "Golden Plate Award for one of the 20th Century's Most Extraordinary Achievers" - an award previously bestowed upon five U.S. Presidents and three Nobel Prize winners

- Accomplished the first "Investment Grade" Wall Street securitization of non-performing unsecured loans

- Acknowledged by BusinessWeek Magazine as "One of the Top 30 Family Friendly Companies" in the United States

- Lauded by Supreme Court Justice, Clarence Thomas for his "Minority Enterprise Initiative"

- Acknowledged by Working Woman Magazine as "One of the Top 100 Best Companies for Working Mothers"

- Appointed by the Governor of Oklahoma to a four year term on the Board of "Oklahoma Futures"

And most definitely, Billionaire Bill Bartmann says, whatever your goals are, "Focus! You can do it!"

Chapter Five - Maintaining Motivation

"Motivation is a fire from within.
If someone else tries to light that fire under you,
chances are it will burn very briefly. "

Stephen R. Covey

We've achieved a lot already! Don't you agree? We've determined our passions, those innermost parts of our core-being that sing to our soul when we give them attention. We've developed goals surrounding these passions, goals that we are totally excited, enthused, and energized about. We've developed a plan of action that will take us closer and closer toward those goals. And we've learned how to focus our attention and cut out the distractions that might take our attention away from our goals, while learning to shift the way we think. We've been very busy! Give yourself a pat on the back. You've come a long way!

Now, since there is a good chance that some of our goals will take a bit of time to achieve, we want to examine how to maintain a high level of motivation over the long haul. After all, we don't want our energy to flag and we don't want to give up just before we reach the finish line, do we?

So think about your primary goal. Now ask yourself, "Why do I want to achieve this goal?" Write it down and answer this question as fully as possible. List every single reason and benefit you can think of, however small or trivial it may seem. Create a clear vivid picture of what it will mean to you to achieve it. The longer your list of reasons for achieving it and the clearer your visual picture, the stronger your focus, your motivation, and your commitment to your goal will be. So put the book down and do this exercise now.

"Why do I want to achieve this goal?"

"When my goal is achieved, where will I be?"

"What will I be doing and saying?"

"How will I be feeling?"

"Who will I be with?"

"What will I look like?"

"What will the achievement look like?"

"When will it be?"

In the last chapter, we talked about surrounding yourself with people who can lift you up and support you in the achievement of your goals. One of the ways to do this is to actually join a networking or support group. For example, if you're working on changing your body shape and are wanting to eat more healthily, it may be a simple matter of contacting your local health food shop or diet group to find like-minded people whose goals are similar to yours.

If your goal is to change your financial situation and you decide after research that you wish to use investment or real estate as a means to achieve that, you can meet with a local (or virtual) group of people who are involved in the same activities and whose goals are similar to yours.

If your goal is to become a writer, then perhaps meet with a writer's group.

If you are unable to find a group of like-minded people to meet with, or if your specific goal does not really lend itself to this type of activity, then consider learning from others that have gone before you.

Jack Canfield aptly stated, "The problem is the average person isn't tuned in to lifelong learning, or going to seminars and so forth. If the information is not on television, and it's not in the movies they watch, and it's not in the few books that they buy, they don't get it." Then again, the average person has not set themselves a goal to bring more passion and balance into their life, either. Consider attending seminars or classes and reading books, with a view to increasing your motivation, learning from those who have gone before you, and possibly finding a mentor, or at least a kindred spirit that you can communicate and share your goals with.

Singer songwriter, Alanis Morrissette said, "I wish that I had reached out for more support when I was younger. I thought I just had to suck it all up, and do everything on my own. I really felt that I was alone, and had that classic thing of 'no one understands me.' If I could tell my then-self what I know now, I'd tell her that there is support all around you. You just have to ask."

Actress, Ellen Barkin offered some very good advice when she said, "Steer clear of anyone who's uncomfortable with you being you. I'd take that further and say, steer clear of anyone who's not proud of you, your accomplishments as a human being, and the things you have yet to accomplish. They should be excited about seeing all of those things unfold."

When you build a network of people, large or small, to assist you in achieving your goals, it becomes easier to maintain motivation. Talk about your plans and tell someone like-minded about them, and you'll notice your level of motivation rising. Strengthen your desire in this manner. Seeing the rewards of your effort clearly motivates you. A good salesman can have you living in your imagined dream home in minutes, and you'll feel motivated to do anything to make it real. Therefore, learn to be your own salesman. Make your dream real.

Former President of the American Psychological Association and founder of the revolutionary 'Positive Psychology' movement, Martin Seligman reminds us, traditional wisdom "holds that there are two ingredients of success . . . the first is ability or aptitude, and IQ tests and SATs are supposed to measure it. The second is desire or motivation. No matter how much aptitude you have, says traditional wisdom, if you lack desire you will fail. Enough desire can make up for meager talent." So do all that you can to strengthen your desire and to sustain it at a high level.

Seligman continues: "I believe that traditional wisdom is incomplete. A composer can have all the talent of Mozart and a passionate desire to succeed, but if he believes he cannot compose music, he will come to nothing. He will not try hard enough. He will give up too soon when the elusive right melody takes too long to materialize. Success requires persistence, the ability to not give up in the face of failure. I believe that optimistic explanatory style is the key to persistence." Which leads us back to that internal locus of control we talked about in the last chapter.

However, in shifting your focus to personal responsibility for the good in your life, it is not necessary or desirable to focus on any perceived weakness you may have. Robert Sternberg, in his book, *Successful Intelligence*, introduces us to the idea that we shouldn't spend too much time focusing on our weaknesses. His research showed that the most successful among us weren't those with the highest IQs or SATs or GPAs. Rather, the most successful are those who know who they are and what they're good at and they focus on developing their strengths.

Seligman concurs: "I do not believe that you should devote overly much effort to correcting your weaknesses. Rather, I believe that the highest success in living and the deepest emotional satisfaction comes from building and using your signature strengths." The same is true in our journey to achieve our goals. Focus on your strengths. In fact, it might be a good thing to write them down in your journal.

My greatest strengths are:

1. _____

2. _____

3. _____

4. _____

5. _____

Consider things like, courage, optimism, creativity, kindness and generosity, tidiness, intelligence, organizational skills, ingenuity, curiosity, open mindedness, good judgment, critical thinking, love of learning, perspective or wisdom, honesty, perseverance, persistence, diligence, industriousness, zest or enthusiasm, love, social skills, teamwork, fairness, leadership, forgiveness or mercy, modesty or humility, discretion, self-control, appreciation of beauty or excellence, gratitude, playfulness, a sense of humor, a strong sense of spirituality, and any others you can think of that might define you.

Put the book down and write your signature strengths now. If you can find a way to use your signature strengths in conjunction with your passions, you have found your calling. Explore ways in which you can use your greatest strengths more often and to their fullest extent. You can now more consciously create a life in which you're using them in greatest service to yourself and to the world. Integrate this idea into any future goal planning.

What are *your* strengths? How are you giving them to something bigger than yourself? We need to become conscious of this as we seek to create a truly good life.

Seligman says, "The good life consists in deriving happiness by using your signature strengths every day in the main realms of living. The meaningful life adds one more component: using these same strengths to forward knowledge, power, or goodness" to others.

So, what are your strengths?

1. _____

2. _____

3. _____

4. _____

5. _____

How are you using them every day?

1. _____

2. _____

3. _____

4. _____

5. _____

And, most importantly, how are you giving them to something bigger than yourself?

_____

_____

_____

T. Harv Eker tells the story of a friend of his who is motivated to slim down. He says:

> Her intention to lose the weight is honest and sincere; desire and action is not the issue. She goes to the gym regularly, participates in multiple softball leagues, and does constant reading on diet trends, trying anything that might work. But eventually, the diet falls by the wayside even if the activities don't, hence her progress fluctuates.

> When I asked what the motivation was for wanting to lose the weight it was, "I'm disgusted with myself." Okay, sometimes pain can be an effective motivator, but how about something a little more . . . self-supportive? I don't know . . . like looking forward to the day you go to the beach and show off? That sounds a little more compelling *and* positively motivating, doesn't it?

> Everyone's motivation is going to be different no matter what the goal, but whatever that "why" is, it better be powerful. It's got to be *emotional*. Hey, sometimes it might even be reacting in a moment of total freak-out, but whatever that trigger is, make it *mean* something to you! **If you have a good enough reason, you'll figure out a way how, won't you?**

Tal Ben-Shahar suggests this exercise: "You are one hundred and ten years old. A time machine has just been invented, and you are selected as one of the first people to use it. The inventor, a scientist from NASA, tells you that you will be transported back to the day when, as it happens, you first read this book. You, with the wisdom of having lived and experienced life, have fifteen minutes to spend with your younger and less experienced self. What do you say when you meet? What advice do you give yourself?"

He reminds us that we *already* know what we need to know to live an incredible life. The challenge is the fact that we rarely bring it into our awareness and then actually *live* from that knowing.

He brings the point home powerfully by describing stories told by people whose lives are transformed when they receive a cancer diagnosis. All of a sudden their lives shift and they start living more in alignment with their deepest values.

Interestingly, Eker continues his previous story with a similar statement:

> I have another friend who quit smoking almost a year now, cold turkey. He had smoked for over 10 years. People, including me, were surprised and proud, all wondering how he did it. No patch. No gum. No electric fake cigarettes. He said it was easy - he looked in the mirror one day and saw a small lump on his neck, in a lymph area.
>
> He then flashed forward to imaginary moments of telling his friends and family that he had cancer. He thought about what it would be like to put them through watching him disintegrate, maybe suffer. He thought about the pain, guilt, and helplessness of those who wouldn't have the strength to deal with all of that.
>
> That small lump turned out to be only a garden-variety in-grown hair, but it was enough. He broke his last cigarettes in half and that was that.

When you have a big enough reason, the "how to's" come a lot more easily. You need clear and powerful reasons. It's also going to allow you to be willing to do whatever it takes.

Cecily MacArthur is an example of just this phenomenon. After having been diagnosed with a serious and life-threatening cancer, she decided that her climb up the corporate ladder had been vain and hollow. Wondering what it was all for, she traded her corporate desk for an office at home, leaving behind the corporate world to become self-employed as a life coach. Developing and strengthening her own spirituality, she now lives a life of passion as a spiritual coach, helping people around the world attune to their higher selves and tap into their own passions.

William James said, "Most people never run far enough on their first wind to find out they've got a second. Give your dreams all you've got and you'll be amazed at the energy that comes out of you."

Don't wait until you have cancer or another life threatening illness to motivate yourself to live an incredible life. Do it now! Live in alignment with your passion!

I am inspired by Veronica Robertson (name changed for protection), a woman who has achieved her dream of becoming a nurse. On the surface, that might appear to be a yawning "so what?" However, to hear the rest of the story is pretty amazing.

Veronica was born to a mother who was an alcoholic and every day of her life her mother made it clear that Veronica was not wanted, was a failed abortion, and that her only purpose in existing at all was to ruin her mother's life. She was not only verbally & mentally abused, but also physically and sexually abused, with all the accompanying horrors. Much of it, she has blocked out and cannot remember, which I am sure is a blessing.

From the age of 10, Veronica expressed a dream that one day she would become a nurse, which expression was thoroughly squashed by every member of her family (not even one supported her!) who said:

- "you'll never do it"
- "white trash don't go to college"
- "blood and guts will only make you sick"
- "you're not smart enough"

and a host of other unsupportive, dream-killing comments.

Of course, as a young adult, Veronica repeated the pattern, marrying an abusive man who gave no regard to her or their two children together. One day she had the courage to decide that she did not want her children growing up the same way she did and when her husband raised his hand to her, with every ounce of bravery she could muster, she grabbed the children and left.

A single mother now responsible for raising two children and paying the bills, she took a job as a stripper and signed up for all the experiences that accompany that environment. She knew going back was not an option but was unhappy where she was, so she had the courage to resurrect her dream of being a nurse.

She worked hard every night stripping her clothes off and receiving abuse, and she scrimped and saved her pennies until she had enough money to enroll at a university on their registered nurse program. She lost a lot of sleep as she went to school full time, worked full time, and raised two children on top of it all. However, through the power of focus, she achieved her dream. After several long years of motivated perseverance, she graduated university with her RN degree and found work as an ICU nurse in which she maintains a very responsible position. She has much to be proud of!

When I asked her if there were times when her motivation flagged, she said, "Sure. But all I had to do was go into the kids' room at night when they were sleeping, and I would look at their little faces, and I knew that I was doing it all for them . . . to give them the life and the mother they deserved." She also said that she worked hard to surround herself with people that would only support her goals and that her 'cheerleaders' would encourage her when her energy was low.

Was it easy leaving behind the abuse she received as a child? Was it easy leaving behind the abuse she received from her husband, to become a single parent, solely responsible for providing a home, paying the bills, and raising two children? Was it easy receiving abuse at work? No. Was it worth it? "Absolutely!" says Veronica.

Veronica Robertson says, "You Can Do It!"

Chapter Six - Overcoming Barriers

The greatest mistake you can make in life is to be continually fearing you will make one.

~Elbert Hubbard

Well, by now you are hopefully beginning to feel like a racehorse at the starting gate. But before you open the gates and commence running your journey, I want to pause for just a moment and have a look at some of the possible barriers that might trip you up. You would likely agree that life can be more like a steeplechase than a sprint around a flat track and to be forewarned is to be forearmed, as the saying goes.

In previous chapters we've talked about the subconscious mind and how we can consciously direct it toward what we want to achieve in life or away from it. Maxwell Maltz said that, "you can use your imagination either constructively or destructively. You are the product of your imagination; win, lose, or draw." He offers the illustration that if a person believes they are stupid, perhaps because that is what they have been told all their life, "then they will act in such a way as to prove to the world that they are stupid."

Brian Johnson said, "We are constantly talking to ourselves. Let's call that our internal dialogue. Imagine something bad happens - whether it's losing your job, or getting in an argument with a friend or spouse. How do you tend to respond? What's your internal dialogue? Some people, the ones who tend to give up easily, habitually say things like: *'It's my fault, it's going to last forever, and it's going to undermine everything I do.'*"

Do you remember that locus of control we talked about? If a person feels like they are a failure in one area of their life and they follow Seligman's formula of permanence, pervasiveness, and personalization, they will then transfer this feeling of failure to the remaining areas of their life and believe that not only is it a permanent condition, but one that is certainly their own fault, as well. By doing so, they thus instruct their subconscious mind to act in accordance with the instructions given ("I'm stupid" or "I'm a failure") and their subconscious replies, "Okay boss! I'll help you in that endeavor!" They then trip over their shoelaces in front of the woman they'd like to ask on a date and they spill coffee all over the sales report just before it is due. After repeated gaffes, they eventually lose their job and say to themselves, "See? I knew I was a failure." The subconscious mind can now pat itself on the back because it has given this person exactly what they have asked for.

In order to achieve our goals, however big or small, we have to believe first, without a shred of doubt in our minds, that we are worthy of them, that we deserve them, and that we are capable of attaining them.

Richard Bach stated that, "you are never given a dream without also being given the power to make it true" or real.

Is there something that you dream of doing, being, or having in your life? Then know that God would not also give you that dream without giving you the power to also make that dream come true. He is not that cruel. In fact, God wants you to succeed! He did not put you here to fail. What would he gain by that?

Og Mandino expressed this thought much better than I ever could in his excellent book, *The Greatest Miracle in the World,* wherein he asks you to imagine that God is sending you a memorandum and this is what the memo says:

Take counsel.

I hear your cry . . .

I have anguished over the cry of a hare choked in the noose of a snare, a sparrow tumbled from the nest of its mother, a child thrashing helplessly in a pond, and a son shedding his blood on a cross.

Know that I hear you, also. Be at peace. Be calm.

I bring thee relief for your sorrow for I know its cause . . . and its cure.

You weep for all your childhood dreams that have vanished with the years.

You weep for all your self-esteem that has been corrupted by failure.

You weep for all your potential that has been bartered for security.

You weep for all your talent that has been wasted through misuse.

You look upon yourself with disgrace and you turn in terror from the image you see in the pool. Who is this mockery of humanity staring back at you with bloodless eyes of shame?

Where is the grace of your manner, the beauty of your figure, the quickness of your movement, the clarity of your mind, the brilliance of your tongue? Who stole your goods? Is the thief's identity known to you, as it is to me?

Once you placed your head in a pillow of grass in your father's field and looked up at a cathedral of clouds and knew that all the gold of Babylon would be yours in time.

Once you read from many books and wrote on many tablets, convinced beyond any doubt that all the wisdom of Solomon would be equaled and surpassed by you.

And the seasons would flow into years until lo, you would reign supreme in your own garden of Eden.

Dost thou remember who implanted those plans and dreams and seeds of hope within you?

You cannot.

You have no memory of that moment when first you emerged from your mother's womb and I placed my hand on your soft brow. And the secret I whispered in your small ear when I bestowed my blessings upon you.

Remember our secret?

You cannot . . .

Let me share with you, again, the secret you heard at your birth and forgot.

You are my greatest miracle.

You are the greatest miracle in the world.

These are powerful words. What he says next has even greater impact.

How could you be a miracle when you consider yourself a failure at the most menial of tasks? How can you be a miracle when you have little confidence in dealing with the most trivial of responsibilities? How can you be a miracle when you are shackled by debt and lie awake in torment over whence will come tomorrow's bread?

Enough. The milk that is spilled is sour . . .

You have been told that you are a special piece of work, noble in reason, infinite in faculties, express and admirable in form and moving, like an angel in action, like a god in apprehension.

You have been told that you are the salt of the earth.

You were given the secret even of moving mountains, of performing the impossible . . .

You are my finest creation.

Within you is enough atomic energy to destroy any of the world's great cities . . . and rebuild it . . .

You have so much. Your blessings overflow your cup . . . and you have been unmindful of them, like a child spoiled in luxury, since I have bestowed them upon you with generosity and regularity . . .

What rich man, old and sick, feeble and helpless, would not exchange all the gold in his vault for the blessings you have treated so lightly . . .

Therefore, I say unto you, count your blessings and know that you already are my greatest creation . . .

Where are the handicaps that produced your failure? They existed only in your mind.

Count your blessings . . .

Consider a painting by Rembrandt or a bronze by Degas or a violin by Stradivarius or a play by Shakespeare. They have great value for two reasons: their creators were masters and they are few in number.

On that reasoning, you are the most valuable treasure on the face of the earth, for you know who created you and there is only one of you . . . Never, until the end of time, will there be another such as you.

One of a kind. Rarest of the rare. A priceless treasure, possessed of qualities in mind and speech and movement and appearance and actions as no other who has ever lived, lives, or shall live.

Why have you valued yourself in pennies when you are worth a king's ransom?

Why did you listen to those who demeaned you . . . and far worse, why did you believe them?

No longer hide your rarity in the dark. Bring it forth. Show the world . . . Proclaim your rarity!

You are my greatest miracle.

You are the greatest miracle in the world.

Og Mandino was a great proponent of ridding your mind of limiting beliefs and science has proven him correct. The person who can rid his mind of limiting thoughts can achieve anything his heart desires!

Limiting beliefs are beliefs that you may have about yourself that are preventing you from getting what you want.

For example, some people have limiting beliefs that they can't get a high-paying job, start their own business, find a loving spouse, travel to exotic destinations, etc.

Now it certainly may require time and focus to get these things, but they are far from impossible!

However, if you have the belief that YOU CAN'T make more money or achieve whatever other dream you have, you won't.

It's as simple as that. You've instructed your subconscious mind that it cannot be done and so it will comply.

Remember the unfounded and limiting belief that it was impossible to run a mile in under four minutes? For decades, it was widely believed that if a man were to try to run faster than one mile in less than four minutes, his lungs would explode. And besides, man can't run that fast anyway. He's just not made that way. It's not possible!

And then Roger Bannister came on the scene and he not only believed that man could run a mile in four minutes, he believed that HE could do it and he set out to prove it to the world. Once Roger Bannister broke the 4-minute mile in 1954 (and shattered the limiting beliefs of runners and countless others around the world) it took only 46 days for another runner to break the 4-minute mile again and even beat Bannister's record.

. . . all because he shattered a limiting belief. What limiting belief is holding you back? What limiting belief do you need to shatter right here and now?

Very few human beings realize the latent potential they have to alter their own lives. They walk in blindness, complaining about outside forces - debt, bad relationships, lack of opportunity, their boss, their parents - while remaining clueless to the power they already possess to alter their current reality.

Everything that's coming into your life, you are attracting into your life and it's attracted by virtue of the images you're holding in your mind. It's what you're thinking about . . . what you're telling your subconscious to go get for you, either by design or unwittingly. Whatever is going on in your mind, you are attracting to you.

So now is the time to clear out any limiting beliefs you may have, including fear.

Children are such a great example in this arena and I have two stories to share with you. The first is told by Film Director, Tracy Trost, about his little daughter, Jocelyn, who was aged three or four at the time.

"We were walking on the beach and she was collecting rocks and she was showing me all these pretty rocks and she was hanging onto these rocks. Pretty soon she had these handfuls of rocks and she could hardly carry them because she had like thirty of them. Then we walked up on this large rock, a beautiful blue rock with a white stripe through it and it was gorgeous. Well, she sees this and she's like, 'Oh I gotta have that.' So she's trying to pick up this big rock but she can't because she's got her hands full with all these small rocks. Every time she bends over a little rock would fall out, so she'll grab that and put it back and she's trying to figure out how to get the big one. I said to her, 'Jocelyn, if you want that big rock, you have to let go of the little rocks.' She didn't want to do it, so we moved on. Finally she turned back. She let go of the little rocks and picked up the big rock and she's happy."

How about you? Are you willing to let go of all your limiting beliefs in order to claim your big goal? It's so worth it!

Sir Ken Robinson tells the story of his four-year-old son in the nativity play. He said the three wise men somehow got muddled up and entered the stage in the wrong order. "I bring you gold", said the first boy with golden curls and a dish-towel on his head. "I bring you myrrh," said the second. The third little boy, handing over his gift, stepped forward and piped up, "Frank sent this!"

Robinson rightly says that, "Kids will take a chance and if they don't know, they'll have a go. They're not frightened of being wrong." He continues, "If you're not prepared to be wrong, you'll never come up with anything original."

Has fear of making a mistake been holding you back from achieving the life you've always desired? If so, shatter that limiting thought right here and right now!

Inventor James Dyson said, "Frustration is my inspiration and making mistakes is my method. I designed a bagless vacuum cleaner because I was annoyed that mine clogged. I then made 5,127 prototypes. The first 5,126 were failures, but I learned something new each time. I kept myself going by following my instincts rather than being guided by experts until I got it right."

Dyson was not afraid to make mistakes.

I once attended a seminar wherein the speaker suggested that there would later be some entertainment and asked the audience if we would rather hear a pianist who had never made a mistake or a pianist who had routinely made thousands of mistakes. Well, it didn't take us long at all to decide, as a group, that we would much rather hear the perfect pianist who does not make any mistakes. The music was going to be beautiful. In fact, we were looking forward to it! The speaker said that he would arrange it for us. "However," he said, "I should warn you that the pianist you have chosen has never been in front of a piano keyboard in his life, nor can he read music."

What! How could that be?

The speaker explained that of course the only reason this pianist had never made a mistake is because he had never even attempted to play the piano. But what about the other pianist, the one who had made thousands of mistakes? She was a concert-level pianist who had recently been invited to play Carnegie Hall. The reason she had made thousands of mistakes was because she was not afraid to attempt new, more difficult pieces and practice every day in an effort to improve her skills. She was working outside her comfort zone and she was not afraid to make mistakes.

F. Wikzek said, "If you don't make mistakes, you're not working on hard enough problems. And that's a big mistake!"

When we move outside of our comfort zone and begin working in our stretch zone where we will have to stretch ourselves and 'up our game,' and learn new skills to become better, it goes without saying that we are going to make mistakes. But that's okay!!! The best and the brightest, the leaders in various fields just pick themselves up, dust themselves off, learn from their mistakes and do it differently next time. How many times did Edison fail before he finally produced a working light bulb? More than one thousand!

A New York Times reporter boldly asked Mr. Edison if he felt like a failure and if he thought he should just give up now. A perplexed Edison replied, "Young man, why would I feel like a failure? And why would I ever give up? I now know definitively over 1,000 ways that an electric light bulb will not work. Success is almost in my grasp."

How about you? Are you willing to scrape your knees more than a thousand times in order to achieve your dreams? More than five thousand times?

"A man should never be ashamed to own he has been in the wrong, which is but saying . . . that he is wiser today than he was yesterday." ~Alexander Pope, in Swift, *Miscellanies*

Are you willing to change your belief system to KNOW unquestioningly and without a doubt that mistakes are not equivalent to failure? Are you willing to believe that mistakes are simply a method for learning better ways to do things? If yes, then welcome to the big leagues. You've just opened the door to a life greater than yourself. (insert smile here)

If you are still doubtful, take a look at what philosopher Brian Johnson had to say on this subject:

It "reminds me of Robert Fritz's brilliant book *The Path of Least Resistance*. He says that the big problem is that we have this conflict between our desire to have something and this equally powerful belief we can't have it/aren't worthy of it/etc. We bounce back and forth between these two poles desperately trying to relieve the tension and not realizing that the only way to do that is to follow [Viktor] Frankl's advice and create a goal worthy of us - a goal that gets us out of bed in the morning and keeps us away from the sedatives we choke ourselves with (from the pills to the TV and the other things we use to 'discharge' that tension). But, news flash: The pain is not going to go away. Not until we commit to our highest self; to a goal worthy of our potential."

Are you willing to let go your fear and commit yourself to a goal worthy of your highest potential?

Johnson mentioned Viktor Frankl, a man with amazing wisdom. Frankl also said, "What is to give light must endure burning." If we are ever to shine brightly, we must first be willing to subject ourselves to the fire. So, how about it? In your endeavor to slay the dragons that are holding you back, are you willing to get a little singed for the reward of a life beyond your greatest expectations? If I smell a little smoke on your clothes, I'll know you answered a resounding, "Yes!"

"The time has come," said Neale Donald Walsch, "for you to have more courage than any war has ever called upon you for, than any hardship has ever demanded, than even suffering has ever required. The time has come for you to confront yourself at the level of belief. The reason this will require so much courage is that your beliefs form the basis of who you think you are. You must challenge yourself. You must challenge your society. You must challenge your world."

Martin Seligman urges us to remember that, "learned optimism is not a rediscovery of the 'power of positive thinking.'" Changing the destructive things you say to yourself when you experience the setbacks that life deals all of us is the central skill of optimism and it is this central skill that will see you achieve your goals. "Pessimists can in fact learn to be optimists, and not through the mindless devices like whistling a happy tune or mouthing platitudes ('Every day, in every way, I'm getting better and better'), but by learning a new set of cognitive skills."

Are you willing to learn a new set of cognitive skills in order to achieve your goals? It's worth it.

Think about your life ten years from now. The choice is yours right now. No matter what path you choose, ten years will have elapsed. You will be ten years older and you will have experienced a few setbacks and some joys. But will you have reached for your dreams? Will you have brought your passions into your life?

You can either be miserable ten years from now, making excuses as to why you never followed your passions, or you can be living your bliss. No matter which choice you make, you will experience bumps in the road along your life's journey. We all will. It is an inevitable fact of life. However, are you going to allow those bumps to be just that? Little roadbumps that you move past? Or are you going to see them as roadblocks that stop you from choosing to pursue your passions?

Mark Victor Hansen admonishes, "Don't wait until everything is just right. It will never be perfect. There will always be challenges, obstacles and less than perfect conditions. So what! Get started now. With each step you take, you will grow stronger and stronger, more and more skilled, more and more self-confident and more and more successful."

Avish Parashar tells the story of the first time his girlfriend entered a triathlon, which had been a dream f hers to do.

> This past weekend, my girlfriend **ran a triathlon**. For those who don't know, a triathlon is a sporting event which people who enjoy self-torture like to do. This was a "Sprint Level" which means that it was a short version (the word "Sprint" implying that people should "sprint" through it or something. Are they crazy, or just bionic?).
>
> By "short," I mean it was made up of an 880 yard swim, a 15 mile bike ride, and a 5K run. Yes, I am aware that those are three different units of measurement. Why do they do that? I'm not sure, but I'm guessing it's to keep the triathletes confused enough to never say, "Hey, we could just use a car and a boat and do this in a fraction of the time."
>
> I mock the triathlon, but in truth, I have wanted to do one for a while. So when my girlfriend came to me and said, "I want to do this triathlon, do you want to do it with me?" I off [sic] course said, **"Not this year"** and went back to drinking my beer.
>
> (Clearly, I need to revisit my own lessons about saying **"Yes, And . . ."**)
>
> ### Part the First: Training
>
> Ignoring my laziness, my girlfriend signed up and started training. **For three months she trained like a madwoman.** Seriously, there was like a "Jekyll and Hyde" thing going on. She never worked out all that regularly before, but once the triathlon training got

under way she became an addict. She never missed a day, and we started scheduling things around her workouts. She even started do additional workouts on her own - and on her "rest" days. Crazy . . .

Part the Second: The Event

The day of the event came and she took off into the water to get started. Once everyone started swimming, I lost track of her. I also somehow missed her as she started the bike portion, so I had no idea where she was. But I kept watch, knowing that the bike course would loop back so I would have to see her eventually.

Time passed. Then more time passed. Then more. And still no sign of her.

I started to get a little worried. Was everything ok? Was she just moving really slowly? Did she get injured? **Did she get a cramp during the swim and drown?!?** (This was one of her worries going into the event, and now it was transferring to me!)

Part the Third: DING!

Then I saw her approaching. Only . . . she was walking her bike. **Uh-oh . . .**

I didn't care at all that she was walking the bike; frankly, I was proud and happy that she signed up and did the damn thing. If she needed to walk part of the bike portion, no big deal. But I wasn't sure *why* she was walking it. Was she tired, or was she injured?

Then I got a glimpse of her face, and she was visibly distraught. **Uh-oh . . .**

I ran up alongside her and asked what happened.

"I got a flat tire," she responded. "I had to walk my bike for the last four miles!"

To be honest, my initial impulse was to burst out laughing. Not because there was anything funny about the situation. It kind of sucked. But I almost laughed because I was so relieved that she wasn't injured. Plus, being a humorist, laughing at things is sort of always my first response.

Being a relatively smart man, I knew that a laugh would have been misinterpreted. So I kept it to myself.

Then I felt bad for her. She had trained so hard for so long and had been looking forward to this day for months, and then she had a major DING! Happen.

That sucks.

After taking an extra forty minutes or so than originally planned, she finally walked her bike across the finish line and moved into the transition area to start the run.

Part the Fourth: The Lesson

As I watched her run off onto the 5K course, I thought to myself, "Wow, I am even prouder of her now than I would have been if she had just finished the triathlon normally."

When that tire went flat, she had two choices.

1. Walk the bike to the finish and then start the run.
2. Quit

The obvious choice is to keep going. But you know as well as I do that when something like that happens, that little voice starts in your head:

- "This is pointless."
- "You may as well give up."
- "You're not meant to do this anyway."

And so on and so on.

The voices would only get stronger as you were forced to slowly walk your bike through the hot sun while rider after rider after rider passed you. All this on your very first triathlon ever.

But she sucked it up, kept going, and did whatever she had to in order to finish the bike segment.

As she moved into the transition area to get ready for her run, she smiled and called out, *"at least I should have no problem with the run now!"*

And that's what it's all about.

"Life inflicts the same setbacks and tragedies on the optimist as on the pessimist, but the optimist weathers them better." Martin Seligman

Think about this: obstacles become stepping stones, once surmounted. By taking baby steps toward your goals, you can deal with seeming obstacles one at a time. Each obstacle that you surmount in this way then becomes a stepping stone, a new platform, from which you can journey forward, stronger, wiser, and taking your next baby step in an upward direction.

Sir Terence Conran, designer, restaurateur, retailer, and a man who has made many mistakes and overcome many obstacles in his career, said, "Don't be afraid of making mistakes . . . Learn from them, adapt to bad situations and emerge on the other side wiser and better equipped for the experience, because if you believe in your ideas, then you must never give up."

The world's greatest sages and teachers universally emphasize that you already contain within you the seeds of greatness. All that you need to know in order to take your next baby step along the path to your dreams, you already know. All the peace, wisdom, and joy in the universe are already within you; you don't have to gain, develop, or attain them. Remember what Vivekananda said? We're like a child standing in a beautiful park with his eyes shut tight. We don't need to imagine trees, flowers, deer, birds, and sky; . . . we merely need to open our eyes and realize what is already here before us and who we really are.

I heard an analogy once that was quite apropos: the idea that life is like a stunning road leading . . . wherever we want to go. The unfortunate thing is that we put a massive 'no entry' sign in our way.

Let's remove that no-entry sign right now! Imagine how you would live your life if you knew that, no matter what, you wouldn't fail. Go on . . . close your eyes and imagine it. What would you achieve?

This is a gentle reminder to live in alliance with your true passion and, very simply, give it a shot! You have nothing to lose. The very worst thing that can happen is that you will wind up ten years from now living the same life you would as if you had never tried. But the very best thing that can happen, and what is much more likely to happen, is that you will be living the life you've always wanted to live, a life full of passion. You honestly *can* have it. And all you have to do to get it is let go of your fear.

Do not be afraid of failure. In discovering your passions, become curious about the things around you and then attempt, learn and attempt again!

John Powell said, "The only real mistake is the one from which we learn nothing."

Singer Morten Harket was once asked in an interview about his unique talent and his reply offers some interesting insight on limiting beliefs and self-esteem. He said, "You can be very talented and have no self-confidence and you will never utter a word or sing a note. That bird will never fly, because it just doesn't dare to do it. It has a stronger voice in it that tells it that if it leaps out of the nest it will plummet to the ground and die. So I'm not sure anymore if talent is something that is just sprinkled on some people. I think we all possess a lot more than we are aware of, and that it is whether or not you believe that you do and you try and open that thing in you that is the main difference between flying or not."

How about you? Are you ready to let go your fear of falling in order to spread your wings and fly?

A sinister sister to the fear of failure is the need to control everything. Both have their roots in fear and low self-esteem. However, if you are ever going to reach your fullest potential, you have to be willing to resign as General Manager of the Universe.

The organization, Alcoholics Anonymous, in their 12-step program, came up with one of the most profound and deepest sayings to ever be released, yet it is also the simplest: 'Let Go, Let God.'

I know it sounds weird, but in order to succeed, we have to give up our desire to control everything and we have to develop a strong faith that the universe will deliver to us all that our heart desires. We have to trust. And it is only when we *do* trust that our dreams will be fulfilled.

Supermodel, actress, and businesswoman Elle MacPherson said, "When I'm obsessing about the outside, it means I'm unhappy on the inside . . . What makes me confident is . . . not trying to control everything."

Wise insight. If you are obsessing with everything on the outside, needing to control everything in your universe, slow down a bit, in fact stop, and take some time to introspect. Look inside yourself and ask, what is it about YOU that you are really trying to control. What is it inside yourself that you are really unhappy with and need to change in order to move forward? Bear in mind that if you avoid this step because of the discomfort factor, you will continue to hold yourself back, unable to achieve your goals until this barrier is removed.

Steven R. Covey said, ""Basing our happiness on our ability to control everything is futile" and he is right, because if our happiness is based on the ability to control other people and circumstances in our lives, we are doomed from the start. We can never be happy because it is impossible to control everyone and everything! People are free agents and they will choose to do whatever they choose to do, regardless of our desire to control them. And the universe will send us whatever circumstances we've programmed our subconscious to get, regardless of our desire for control. That's just the way it works. In fact, I'll bet God finds it really funny and actually laughs out loud at us trying to manipulate everything and control the vast universe to bend it to our will.

Why not just let go and let God provide you with the very best He has to offer? Trust Him to bring you your dreams and goals and resign as General Manager of the Universe.

Bob Proctor agrees and says that, "thoughts that would otherwise be obsessed with the negative event can now be redirected and focused on something positive."

When we're not stressing over the universe refusing to be controlled by us, we actually free up our mental energies to think about more positive things . . . like our passions. And we leave ourselves with the mental faculty to be able to redirect our thoughts and control the work of the subconscious mind. So if you feel a need to control something, there is a good thing to focus on . . . controlling the direction of your subconscious, instead. You'll be glad you did.

As long as we're learning to let go, let's talk about forgiveness.

Remember what Maxwell Maltz said? "You can use your imagination either constructively or destructively. You are the product of your imagination; win, lose, or draw."

"Yes," you say, "but you don't know my background."

It makes no difference. We all come from somewhere that could have been better and we've all done things in the past we wish we could change, successful people and unsuccessful alike. Brian Tracy said, "It doesn't matter where you are coming from. All that matters is where you are going."

Continuing to hold onto negative feelings, either toward yourself in the form of guilt or toward others in the way of blame, is destructive. It will prevent you from moving forward in life or achieving your goals as surely as tying a one ton ball and chain around your ankle would. It sets up a negative thought process that becomes a vicious cycle and directs your subconscious along the wrong path.

Learn to let go your guilt and blame. If you need help offloading baggage, consider seeking the expertise of a professional. You'll only liberate yourself to move forward by doing so.

TV personality, music manager, and promoter, Sharon Osbourne, said, "I don't hold grudges. They take up too much emotion and space. It's not good to hold onto things and build on them. You're not free if you wake up and have negative thoughts going through your head, when you could be doing something positive and good instead. Letting go of bitterness is liberating."

Model and actress, Jerry Hall, agreed when she said, "You don't have to let family patterns repeat themselves. You can take control . . . You have to create the environment you want to live in."

Breaking that chain of destructive behavior not only frees you to move forward and create a better future for yourself, it creates a better future for generations to come, setting a positive example for others to model.

Syrus said, "From the errors of others, a wise man corrects his own" and Mark Victor Hansen said that a "lack of forgiveness causes almost all of our self-sabotaging behavior." Why would you want to sabotage yourself and your chance of achieving your goals? Learn from both the mistakes and successes of others. Let go of guilt and blame and learn to forgive.

"We want scapegoats, forgetting that we are all capable of wrongdoing and that when we punish and humiliate others, we are actually punishing and humiliating ourselves. Forgiveness - and pardon - are the things that enable us to escape the past and create a humane future." - Alexander McCall Smith, author of The Lost Art of Gratitude

Henry David Thoreau said, "One cannot too soon forget his errors and misdemeanors; for to dwell upon them is to add to the offence." I would also add that one cannot too soon forgive and forget the errors and misdemeanors of others. Carrying around baggage that heavy only weighs a person down. Letting go, a person's life is all the happier for it.

Are you able to forgive and let go? If you are not, then who holds the power - you or the person you are unwilling to forgive?

When you make a choice to forgive others, you are not lying down and becoming a doormat, nor are you saying the other person is in the right. Forgiveness is about letting go of the past so that it no longer controls your present and your future. It is also taking back control of your life and not allowing your negative emotions to direct your subconscious mind's work. And finally, forgiveness is also about letting go of all those debilitating emotions that could be responsible for sabotaging your current relationships! So ask yourself this question: Do you want to feel good? If you are still carrying feelings of resentment and anger toward someone else, then what are you getting out of it?

Examine what rewards you are getting by hanging onto your limitations or barriers. Is it attention, sympathy, something else? Ask yourself, "Which do I want more: the rewards that I gain from hanging onto my limiting thoughts or beliefs? Or the rewards that come from achieving my goals and dreams, from truly living a passionate life?" It is crunch time. You must decide, as the choice is totally yours and no one else can make the decision for you.

Hanging on to feelings of resentment, hatred or anger, will ensure that these destructive feelings *will* spill over into your current life and stop you from enjoying positive, successful relationships with other people, as well as impede the general enjoyment of life.

The fact is, your subconscious mind never ignores negative energy and emotions. It will remind you every day that you need to deal with them by manifesting more negative in your life. It's a heat-seeking missile, remember? Until you do deal with your negative baggage, your subconscious mind will manifest your unresolved emotional pain through insomnia, chronic physical pain and in extreme cases, through life threatening illness. It can also manifest itself through erratic and irresponsible behavior and in a desire to experience numbness. Remember the addictive sedatives Brian Johnson spoke of (TV, drugs, alcohol, sex, etc.)?

So there it is; make a decision today to take back your life by practicing forgiveness . . . of yourself and others. Your energy is extremely precious, so don't allow yourself to give it away through hanging onto negative emotions! Move on with your life today and begin to experience miracles.

Brian Tracy said, "The happiest people in the world are those who feel absolutely terrific about themselves, and this is the natural outgrowth of accepting total responsibility for every part of their life." Actor, Mickey Rourke, agreed when he said, "It wasn't until I took responsibility for myself that things started to change."

Which is another reminder to change that locus of control and shift our focus.

Accept responsibility for where you are today. Most people don't take personal responsibility for their present results. They honestly believe the cause of their current results lies outside of themselves, due to conditions or circumstances they have no control over. But we know now this is not the case. Remember the locus of control?

Donna Johnson tells the story of running into an old friend and the effect it has had on her life:

> Recently I was reacquainted with a close friend that I hadn't seen in over twenty years. This person reminded me of many things I had said years ago concerning my future. It was shocking to have some of my thoughts brought back as we reflected over the past. In some ways, it was apparent that I had followed a focused course to accomplish many things in my life. In other ways, it was evident that somewhere along the road I embraced limitations in certain areas of my life. After that conversation, which was the beginning of many more, I realized I hadn't just changed my dreams and goals. Something else had happened. I found myself asking certain questions over and over. When did I stop believing certain things were possible? When did I start limiting myself in certain areas? When did I stop expecting certain things out of life? When did I convince myself that those things were not for me? Were there external and/or internal forces at work? Should I shake these feelings or allow myself to search for the answers? Do I want to know the answers?

We know now that the outcomes we get in life are a direct result of what we tell our subconscious minds to get.

So as Donna Johnson rightly suspected, if you don't like the results in your life, you need to change your thoughts. Bob Proctor states, "This is an orderly universe. Nothing happens by accident. The images you plant in your marvelous mind instantly set up an attractive force, which govern your results in life."

Are you too old to achieve your dream? Then listen to what Diana Athill (age 91) had to say: "If you catch yourself thinking 'what's the point at my age' squash it!" Now there's a woman who knows how to enjoy life!

I could list every possible excuse a person could make for not going after their goals and every possible reason a person should dismiss those excuses. And this would become a very long book, indeed.

Truthfully, it doesn't matter what barrier might hold you back from achieving your goals. The way to overcome your barriers is to change your thoughts . . . in all cases. No exceptions. When you master this concept, you become the master of your own destiny.

Neale Donald Walsch said that "if you saw you as God sees you, you would smile a lot" and your limiting beliefs would disappear. Learn to see yourself as God sees you. Learn to see yourself as unlimited.

I am inspired by the story of my friend, Jim Stovall who has done more to prove that you too can do it than anyone else I know.

He was told one day in his young adult life by three different doctors, "Jim, we're not sure why and we're not exactly sure when, but we do know that someday you <u>will</u> be totally blind and there's not one thing we can do about it."

Upon receiving this news, Jim said his whole world just stopped. He had no clue what he was going to do. Unable to deal with this earth-shattering event, he just pretended like it was never going to happen, because he couldn't deal with it.

"Did you ever know anybody," Jim asks, "who is going 80 miles an hour straight toward a brick wall and they act like nothing bad is ever going to happen? Well that was me. I had a marvelous capacity for burying my head in the sand."

He enrolled in college and near his college there happened to be a school for blind children.

"To this day, I don't know what my motives were, whether I was trying to make a deal with God or help out, or learn more about it, or what, but I went over to this school for blind children and I met with the principal and I said look, I'm seventeen years old, I have no background, no training, no experience in working with blind kids, but I'd like to teach here. Well, you can imagine how excited they were to see me."

"Oh yeah," mimics Jim, "Here's the guy we've been looking for right here!"

But the school did tell Jim that if he was serious about wanting to help out, they did have one kid he could work with, a four-year-old boy named Christopher who was not only blind, but also had challenges with motor skills and other physical problems.

"Okay. What do I teach this kid?" he asked.

"Well, that's just it," the Principal said. "*We have determined that he's never going to grow or learn or advance or develop any more than he already has.* So what we want you to do is to keep Christopher quiet and away from the other kids so that they can learn their lessons."

Jim wishes to emphasize here that we **always** live up to the expectations that we have of ourselves or those expectations that we allow other people to place upon us and he is so right on target with that.

While looking forward to working with Christopher, the only training Jim received in this new teaching endeavor was to be told by the principal, "Keep his shoelaces tied; we're afraid he's going to trip over them. And don't let him go near the stairs. Blind people have a problem with stairs. Other than that, we don't care what you do. Just keep him quiet so the other kids can learn their lessons."

"Well, that first day," Jim recounts, "I went out to meet Christopher and he was very, very small, much smaller than you would expect a four-year-old to be. And I said to him, before I leave here, no matter how many days or weeks or months or years it takes, you are going to at least learn how to tie your shoes and climb the stairs. And he said, 'No. I can't.' And I said, 'Yes, you can.' And he said, 'No. I can't.' And I said, 'Yes . . . you can!' And he said, 'No! I can't!' And if you've ever spent any time with a four-year-old child, you know that this can go on all day. But I had never experienced anything quite like that. 'No, I can't.' 'Yes, you can.' No, I can't.' Yes, you can.' It wears you right down," Jim said with a wry smile.

133

So Jim attended university every day and worked with Christopher every afternoon, learning how to tie shoes and climb stairs. And true to the doctor's word, one day Jim Stovall hit that brick wall at 80 miles an hour and woke up one morning unable to see, unable to read or study his university books.

"I didn't know what you know right now," Jim states. "I didn't know that I could exercise my right to choose and make a quality decision to change my life by changing my mind. I would have given a million dollars that day to know what you know right now because it's been worth a lot more than that to me in every area of my life since then."

"But I didn't know that. So I did the only thing I was prepared to do and that was quit."

Jim went into the principal's office to tell him that he would no longer to be able to teach Christopher and that he would also need to drop out of college.

"I didn't know they had dropped Chris off early that day," Jim recalls. "And Christopher was standing outside the open door to the office, hearing this whole conversation. So, as I went out to tell him goodbye and that I love him and tell him that I hope someday someone else would come and work with him, he turned to me and said, 'Yes, you can.' And I said, 'No. I can't.' And he said, 'Yes! You can!' I said, 'No. I can't!' He said, 'Yes! You can!'"

"And as I was preparing to explain to this poor, ignorant, uninitiated, uniformed four-year-old child how this was somehow different, kid, this was not like learning how to tie your shoes . . . this was like going to a major university . . . as I was preparing to explain this so that he could understand, it hit me like a ton of bricks: Stovall, you either need to get up and do something with your life or quit lying to this kid, because if it works, it works for tying your shoes and climbing the stairs, and finishing college, and creating lives and careers and businesses and lifestyles and destinies that are worthy of you and worthy of your best efforts. And if it doesn't work, then let's quit lying to people."

Three years later, Jim Stovall graduated from that university with honors and with not one, but two, degrees and that very same week, he had the privilege of seeing with what little vision he had left, ("In fact it's one of the last things I really remember seeing," he says.) his little friend Christopher, who was now aged seven, climb three flights of stairs by himself, turn and sit on the top step and tie both of his shoes.

"And that is the person who has impacted my life the most. It's not all the movie stars [I've worked with], the athletes, the millionaires, the billionaires. It's a four-year-old child that came into my life for three years to teach me the unadulterated wisdom of the ages, which is quite simply this: No matter what the dream is inside of you, the answer is always 'Yes, you can!' because that big dream would not have been put inside of you if you did not have the capacity to achieve it."

Jim emphatically says, "I don't know your name. I don't know where you're from. I don't know the challenges and the obstacles and the barriers that you face in your world, in your business, in your career, or in your personal life, but there is one thing I know about you and about your big dream. There is one thing I know about that, better than you know about yourself and that is quite simply this: when it comes to that big dream, the biggest one you ever had inside of you, **it always too soon to quit.** You think you've tried everything. You think you've thought of everything. You think you're at the end of your rope. You're not even close! And I hope that enough obstacles and challenges and barriers will come into your world so that you will find out what a giant of a human being you were created to be."

Does Jim Stovall believe? Absolutely! Jim says, "You can do it!"

Chapter Seven - Using Your Intuition

Whenever I experience any kind of setback, I always pick myself up and try again . . . Look outside the box and try and find a solution. You'll be surprised how many great opportunities and possibilities arise when things look bad. You've just got to open your mind and not be afraid of sticking your neck out . . . Fear is the only thing that stops people acting intuitively and going with their gut.

Richard Branson

According to the dictionary, intuition is the act or faculty of knowing or sensing without the use of rational processes; immediate cognition. Psychiatrist Carl G. Jung, in Psychology Types (1923) described intuition as "a perception of realities which are not known to the conscious, and which goes via the unconscious."

Christian Carter describes it similarly. "It's the idea that you instinctively know more about what's going on in the world around you than you or your conscious mind fully recognizes."
Yet somehow, that doesn't quite describe the *power* or *impact* intuition can have in our lives when we learn to tap into it and use it to best advantage.

Louise Hay said, "We are far more than we allow ourselves to be. 'Second Sight' helps you understand this."

José Silva and Burt Goldman said that "when you understand the mechanism of the mind, you can control your life better." So in order to control our lives better, let's see if we can grasp this thing called intuition.

The intellect (our rational thinking mind) requires intuition to function at maximum performance. In other words, our capacity to reason can only get us so far. Intuition, Jung said, is not merely a perception, but a creative process with the capacity to inspire. By adding intuition to our intellect, we create a synergistic effect where one plus one does not equal two. It equals three or four or more. We add to our logic a creative process with the capacity to understand anything far better than solely our rational mind could and with the enormous capacity to inspire . . . both ourselves and others!

According to Carter, "intuition is something that comes pre-wired in your brain. The way your conscious and subconscious mind is hooked up to the rest of your complex body systems and senses make it possible. So the good news is that this ability is there for you anytime you want to use it. But the bad news is that you have to take time to fully tune into it and recognize your ability."

"Entrenched patterns," Charles W. McCoy Jr. said of the logical mind, "become extremely difficult to change, as Galileo discovered when he suggested, counter to Church dogma, that the earth does not occupy the center of the universe." The head of the Church was thinking with his logical, rational mind, while Galileo was using his intuitive mind.

Traditionally trained physician, Judith Orloff states that "intuition is a potent form of inner wisdom not mediated by the rational mind. It can be experienced as a flash of insight, a gut feeling, a hunch, a sensation of energy, or a dream . . . It will help you make decisions that inwardly feel right and reconnect with what you really care about. Finding your inner voice can give you the confidence and wisdom to face anything; following it is key to living a passionate, high-energy life."

Have you ever heard a wee quiet voice in your head telling you to do or not do something?

"Don't sign that contract! You'll be sorry!"

"Quick!!! Get off the freeway!!!"

"You need to go see the doctor."

Often this inner voice will give us messages of safety, telling us things that, if we listen to them, will either save our lives or our health. In this situation, people will usually say they 'had a gut feeling,' however unexplained, 'a knowing' that, if asked, they would not have been able to substantiate.

On the day of the September 11th 2001 World Trade Center incident, for example, an unusually large number of people reported a feeling of dread before going to work in New York City. Why is that? Intuition. Those people had 'a hunch' that something bad would happen that day.

Karim Hajee tells a personal story, an experience that I've had myself on the very same freeway! He says:

> Several years ago I was in Seattle - a city I'm somewhat familiar with but not completely knowledgeable of all the streets. I recall driving along near Pike Place Market - trying to figure out how to get back on to Interstate 5 and head north. Finally I figured out how to get back on the freeway - and decided to speed up a little. The car in front of me was going rather slow so I thought about passing it - but something didn't sit right - so I just stayed behind him. A minute later another car zipped past us both. It was not more than 20 feet ahead of us going through a green light when another car smashed into it. The other car was going through a red light. We had to stay and talk to the police, but my instincts saved me! That could have been me in the accident had I chosen to pass the car a minute earlier - but I trusted my gut and stayed put.

How about you? Have you had an experience like Hajee's where your intuition saved you from danger? It's not uncommon.

But saving us from danger is not intuition's only function and, when used solely for this purpose, is under-utilizing a tremendous resource . . . sort of like using a directed trickle from the Colorado River to water your garden, not realizing that it also has the capacity to forge the Grand Canyon for you.

So what else can intuition do? Hay, Jung, and Orloff have already alluded to its creative abilities. However, Vishen Lakhiani, gives a bit greater insight when he says that "there are 4 levels of intuition. Level 1 is your warning system. Level 2 revolves around your social intuition. Level 3 is your creative intuition and level 4 is higher purpose intuition."

We've already discussed your early warning system a bit and if you haven't yet tapped into that and begun using it, I would highly recommend you do! It could just save your life!

But what is this level 2 social intuition Lakhiani talks about?

Social Intuition is a highly attuned function found commonly in twins and also in people who have empathetically learned to sense the moods and thoughts of those they are emotionally close to, like a mother sitting in the living room, sensing that her son on the other side of the globe is in danger. Or one twin finishing the other's sentences. The best of the world's leaders have developed this type of intuition and when utilized in business as a means of sensing the thoughts and moods of staff and customers, or even competitors, serves managers well.

Deborah Allen tells the story of her daughters' intuition:

> When my identical twin girls, Ashley and Rachael, were about a month old, Rachael developed a very

high temperature. I took her to the doctor and he immediately admitted her to hospital. As I had another baby and a two year old at home I was unable to stay with Rachael at the hospital. The first night away from home Rachael was very restless and would not settle. Ashley was the same, she just would not settle. The next night was the same.

As Rachael was still unwell, the doctor decided to keep her in hospital for another night, but asked if I could take Ashley to the hospital and leave her there that night to see if either of the girls would settle. They both slept soundly all night! The staff at the hospital were amazed. It appeared that at such a young age the girls knew their sister was not there! The girls [normally] slept in separate bassinets on opposite sides of my bed.

My girls are now 16 and are still extremely close. They share the same room still and they have the same group of friends. They sometimes appear to communicate to each other without talking (although they don't realize that they do it) and they often finish each other's sentences or answer questions for each other.

This mental telepathy Allen describes is a form of social intuition and is not just restricted to twins.

B. Andrews of White Plains, New York tells an embarrassing story of a colleague's use of social intuition:

I work for an advertising agency as a copywriter and I want to relay my experiences with a graphic artist, which never fail to astonish me.

Her name is Angel and she is truly an angel.

The way we work it here in the office is I'm given an assignment, usually a product for which to create an ad. I'll write the copy, then arrange a meeting with Angel so she can do the artwork.

Our mission is to create an ad or ads that people will be drawn to and remember. When I first sit down with Angel, I am usually geared up to present her with my ideas, but most of the time she simply picks up on my thoughts and starts sketching ideas that I have in my mind.

I don't know how she does it, but time after time she usually hits it on the mark. She has the ability to climb inside my head, and it's both fascinating and unnerving.

One minor problem is she is quite beautiful and sexy, but we stay careful not to get personal as our company has strict policies about 'extra-curricular' activities. The problem, of course, is sometimes I can't take my eyes off her and she knows exactly what I'm thinking. I mean to the last detail, if you know what I mean.

It has happened more than once when I have a vision of the two of us in a compromising position, and she has whispered in my ear, "Nice thought but forget it buster."

Fortunately she has a good sense of humor, but it is unnerving knowing she can sense what I am envisioning. It helps in creating an advertising campaign but embarrassing when I'm thinking of 'other' things.

I guess Andrews forgot to keep his 'business hat' on.

One final example of social intuition in the workplace and then we'll move on to level 3. Mark DeMoss, CEO of The

DeMoss Group, had a strong connection with his social intuition. He wanted to create a strong company with happy employees, like any good CEO would. Being in tune with his intuition, DeMoss sensed "that without good people - trusted, professional, respected, motivated, inspired, rested people - I have no firm." His intuition told him that after five years of dedicated hard work his employees needed a sabbatical and that he should give them five weeks off work to rest and have recreation.

His rational mind reasoned that this was just not possible. The company would suffer financially, his clients would miss key people and go to another firm, the added workload would be stressful for other staff, etc. There were any number of logical reasons he could think of not to give his employees an extended vacation.

Yet, on a leap of faith he decided to trust his intuition and when his first employee (the VP of the company, Beth) approached her five year anniversary, he announced his plans to all staff members. They were each to be given a five week paid vacation on their fifth anniversary, in which they were to have no contact with the company, were not allowed to take work with them, nor could they stay in touch with staff while they were away. It was intended to be a true vacation. "In return," DeMoss said, "I asked only that the person taking a sabbatical commit to spend at least one more year with us."

"Beth used her time away that year to hike the north coast of Maine, visit family and friends in North Carolina and Virginia, and spend time doing nothing at all. Meanwhile," DeMoss said, "I confess that until she walked back in the front door - our first experiment in this perk - I hadn't realized that I could hold my breath for five weeks. During that time, we didn't speak once. To my delight, the wheels of the firm rolled on as the team deftly covered Beth's client work (realizing others would do the same for them when their sabbatical rolled around). Just as sweet was Beth's summary statement on her weeks away: 'The timing was impeccable, you'll never know,' she said, blowing in these days with fresh winds and new energy. She thanked me as if I'd known all along that like a car stuck in stop-and-go city traffic, after five years a person needs to flush the buildup in her mental engine."

Looking at statistics, we see that 40 percent of all America's workers feel disconnected from their employers; two-thirds come to work with scant motivation to help achieve their employers' business goals or objectives; 25 percent admit to showing up just to collect a paycheck. Little wonder then that DeMoss was very glad that instead of following logic and reason, and inadvertently allowing his best resources to burn out, he listened to his social intuition.

So how about you? Are you learning to listen to and trust your own social intuition?

In a study conducted by Professor John Mihalasky of the New Jersey Institute of Technology, it was found that CEOs who performed best in tests of intuition also tended to be the ones with the highest profit growth over the course of 5 years in their respective businesses. In fact, the results were stunning.

Over 81% of the CEOs who obtained a high score on Mihalasky's intuition test increased their company's profitability by over 100% within 5 years.

In comparison, approximately 25% of those who scored average and below average on Mihalasky's intuition test managed to do the same.

These findings point to one clear conclusion: Having a high intuitive ability makes you a whopping 226% better at making money than those who don't! If that isn't incentive to develop your social intuition, I don't know what is!

- If you're working in a sales role, social intuition can help you detect the thoughts and needs of your prospects better.

- If you're working in a non-sales role, intuition will help you develop innovations and do your job better.

- If you're in a managerial role, you'll certainly be able to manage your team much more insightfully, as Mark DeMoss' example illustrates.

- If you're in a customer service role, social intuition will help you discern win-win solutions for both the customer and the company.

- If you run your own business, intuition will help you make better decisions with regard to long term strategy and short-term goals.

Level 3 intuition is called creative intuition. Successful inventors, entrepreneurs, artists, designers, writers, and others have, to their great credit, learned to tap into and pay close attention to this type of intuition.

Thomas Edison once said that "ideas come from space." When they did for him, he was in tune with his creative intuition.

Creative intuition is that intuition which, not only brings us brilliant ideas, ideas our logical mind could never come up with on its own, but also streamlines the creative process for us, aiding us in solving difficult problems, creating art and music, designing things, including engineering or architectural designs, and becoming more attuned to our own feelings and the health of our relationships.

Lakhiani says that "history is filled with countless stories of how creative intuition has aided in the creation of inventions, art, and designs. Even businesses have grown and flourished because of intuition." Microsoft, Apple, and Google are modern examples of just that. He tells the story of Elias Howe, the inventor of the sewing machine:

"He was struggling for years to come up with the design for the sewing machine needle. One night he had a dream where he was surrounded by cannibals who were holding spears with holes in them. This gave him the idea that the thread hole for the sewing needle had to be at the tip of the needle and not at the top.

That was how the sewing machine was invented."

When Shari Repasz Schwendener created her dance suite, '128', she said in March 2005, "The idea came to me in a traffic jam on 128 - not that I would create a dance suite, but looking at ALL the huge cars with only one perfectly groomed person [in each car] with all the 'right' things . . . cell phones, note pads, sharp clothes, perfect hair. Then it hit me, IT isn't about the stuff, it's about why we are HERE. Our relationships, the causes we make. Over the next 9 years, through conversations, observations and growing, '128' has morphed into what you see tonight."

When Shari was sitting in that nasty snarl of traffic, did she realize that tapping into her creative intuition would later yield, arguably, her best work to date?

How about you? Are you accessing your creative intuition on a frequent basis?

Finally, we arrive at level 4 intuition, that which is known as your Higher Purpose intuition. Lakhiani states that, "This is the most useful and the most amazing level of intuition. At this level, your subconscious mind works with you and your intuition guides you to move towards your life purpose. People with this ability are amazingly successful in the stock market or business. Take a look at Sir Richard Branson; he works with over 300 partners, yet he knows within 60 seconds of meeting a person whether to establish a professional relationship or not."

A person that is well in tune with this type of intuition will be working in alignment with what (s)he knows to be his or her divine mission in life. It is very common for this type of person to meditate daily, to listen intently to that inner voice when making decisions and to trust that their intuition will guide them in the proper direction. They do this with a firm knowing and a sense of purpose. Lakhiani rightly states that a person who is living to his full potential uses their subconscious mind to give them the momentum and the push they need to help them complete their life's purpose. They are highly intuitive beings that are making a maximum impact on the world.

Wow! That's powerful stuff! If you'll think back to earlier chapters, we spoke about creating a network of people who can help you get to your goals. I highly recommend including a few Higher Purpose intuitives in your network for maximum impact! These people can not only help you get to where you want to go, they can help you to get there fast and inspire you along the way!

So let's bring this discussion on intuition home, right to our front doorstep.

"How can I personally learn to tap into my own intuition? How can I develop it so that it is so strong, there's no mistaking it for my imagination?"

Good questions! And I'm glad you asked!

If you would like to tap into this hidden power within you, there are several things you can do to develop your various intuitions.

If you followed my earlier advice to take up meditation, then you are likely beginning to already experience some of its benefits. University of Arizona's Stuart Hameroff, MD, said that "when you meditate and attain nothingness . . . it isn't quite nothingness. You move more deeply into the basic fabric of the universe and actually become more consciously a part of it."

However, here is where you will receive great serendipity: in the area of increased intuition. Why?

Because of the way your brain works or functions. If a medical professional were to connect you up to an EEG (electro encephalogram), they would be able to measure your brainwaves in CPS (cycles per second). The CPS would range anywhere from .5 (half a cycle) for a person in deep sleep (known as a Delta state) to 85 cycles per second for a person experiencing an epileptic seizure.

According to Brian Johnson, "The normal higher end is closer to 40 CPS" and he offers this chart for a more complete understanding:

Brain States		
Type	CPS	Qualities
Delta	½ - 4	- Deep, unconscious sleep
Theta	5-7	- Deep, comfortable sleep
Alpha	8-13	- REM sleep - Meditation - Health restoration
Beta	14-40	- Conscious, aware state > 21 CPS = stress, anxiety < 19 CPS = genius creativity

"First, know that the higher our brain waves' CPS, the more agitated we are," Johnson says. "We're stressed any time our CPS goes over 21. Knowing this, we (obviously) want to avoid hanging out at > 21 CPS. How? Start by recognizing the fact that there's an absolute correlation between how quickly our brain is moving (as measured by our CPS), how quickly our thoughts are jumping around, and how much agitation/inability to focus/stress we're experiencing."

Intuition is incredibly difficult to tap into when our brainwaves are operating at a frequency of greater than 21 cycles per second. In fact, even any kind of rational thinking becomes difficult when our brainwaves are operating at greater than 21 CPS . . . and the higher the cycles per second, the more difficult it is to think clearly. We lose not only the ability to tap into our intuition, but also our ability to reason. Ever see a person fly into a rage?

In order to access our intuition, we need to slow our brainwaves down to between 4 and 14 CPS and meditation is an excellent way to do that.

Hajee says, "You can hardly open a major news publication these days without seeing yet another scientific study raving about the incredible benefits of meditation. Meditation has been proven to extend your life . . . create more happiness . . . increase inner peace . . . lower stress levels . . . increase mental clarity . . . and resolve long-standing emotional problems, including fear, anxiety, depression, anger, and substance abuse."

It will also lower the frequency of your brainwaves.

In addition to meditation, build relaxation into your lifestyle as much as possible. Many a brilliant business idea has been spawned on the golf course, after all.

Find as many ways as possible to just generally slow down and relax. Even if it's simply a hot bubble bath at the end of the work day or a walk in the park on the weekend.

When you get into the habit of leading a slower-paced, more relaxed life, mentally, and not allowing your thoughts to jump all over the place, you can begin to recognize intuitive thoughts and messages coming to you from a variety of sources. Engage your five senses (and beyond). Recognize that any of our senses can be utilized to intuitively receive information.

Let's assume that you are working to solve a problem. Slow the frequency of your brainwaves down, then use your logical, reasoning mind to ask the question. (for example, "How can I get little Johnny to willingly WANT to do his homework every night?") After you ask the question, . . . sense . . . listen . . . watch . . . feel . . . even taste and smell for information.

It is possible the answer may come to you right away in the form of 'knowing'. What often happens, though, is that later that day (or the next day) we will see an article in the newspaper that just so happens to directly answer our question or we will be having a conversation with someone who 'coincidentally' happens to mention that their kid just loves to do homework.

We hear a song on the radio or see a film that speaks directly to us, in answer to our question. A random road sign. A scent that causes us to recall a long-forgotten memory, which memory happens to be the answer we were looking for. A sound of water dripping or a pen clicking. You never know.

Billionaire Bill Bartmann uses this technique to his advantage frequently. He states, "I have a process that I employ that has been extremely beneficial to me. When I don't know something that I really want to know, when I can't figure out the answer to a dilemma or a question, when I go to bed at night, I charge my subconscious with solving the problem. I literally talk to my subconscious and pass the problem on to it. 'Hey look, I'm tired. I'm going to bed, I need some sleep, but here's the problem. Here's what I'd like you to do: I'd like you to help me solve this issue. I don't know what it's going to look like, but think on this and give me an answer in the morning. I'm going to bed. Good night.' And here's the uncanny part: Most of the time, I wake up with the idea, I wake up with the suggestion, I wake up with the answer. Now not every time, not always, not infallibly, not 100%, but the grand majority of the time, I wake up with the conscious thought of, 'Huh. That's what I need to do!'"

In an internet forum's discussion on intuition, one man stated that he felt like he really needed to get in touch with a friend he had lost contact with. "That night," he said, "I went to sleep and dreamed that I was in a car and saw my friend across the road. I called her name and waved and made a sign for her to telephone me. The next day she called. I have had several dreams of this nature, which usually occur when (before going to sleep) I ask to be given a dream in answer to a dilemma or decision I have to make."

Intuitive answers can come from any variety of sources. You can dismiss them as coincidence and therefore close your mind to them or you can accept them as answers from the universe, or an unexplained method of 'knowing things' and encourage your intuition to strengthen itself.

If you wish to begin working in alignment with your higher purpose, I would recommend following Branson's example and develop your sensitivity to what is within you by allowing your intuitions to take center stage, instead of dismissing them.

Bill Harris said, "The human brain has the quality of plasticity or malleability throughout life - if it receives the kind of stimulation that allows it to grow and adapt." The same holds true for developing intuition.

Slowing down your mind and tuning in to signals, thoughts, and feelings are the keys. Silva and Goldman state that "as with any endeavor, you will improve as you practice. Improvement in this case means that ultimately you will simply close your eyes, take a deep breath, and be at [a] level" where you can readily access your intuitive responses.

The more you enjoy your meditation, the quieter your mind will become. The happier and more relaxed your mind is, the easier and more natural your receiving will be.

Most of us are aware that our brains are composed of a right hemisphere and a left hemisphere and that each hemisphere in the brain serves a different purpose (from the other). Generally speaking, the left hemisphere of the brain is designed for logical, organizational types of thinking and tasks, while the right side of the brain is used for creative tasks as well as bonding and relationship-strengthening.

Left hemisphere functions include linear reasoning, language functions such as grammar and vocabulary, numerical computation, and direct fact retrieval.

Stephen Simpson says that the creative hemisphere of the brain, "the right brain, is the part of the brain that musicians need to access to be in the groove, where great speakers find their flow, and where athletes get in the zone. The zone is that magical place where things become easy . . . where we feel very relaxed and confident." It's a great place to be. And, not coincidentally, the right brain is where you will also find your intuition.

According to G. Vallortigara, specialization of the two hemispheres is common in vertebrates including fish, frogs, reptiles, birds and mammals, with the left hemisphere being specialized to categorize information and control everyday, routine behavior, and the right hemisphere responsible for responses to novel events and behavior in emergencies including the expression of intense emotions.

"The innate duality of the brain is made more acute," Harris says, "by the fact that in virtually all people, the two hemispheres are unbalanced, a state called *brain lateralization* . . . The greater the lateralization of the brain, the greater the feelings of separation - and the greater the feelings of separation, the greater the stress, anxiety, and isolation."

In order to successfully employ whole-brained thinking (including the use of intuition), you will need to reduce lateralization to the greatest extent possible and, according to Harris, the best way to do that is through meditation. His work in this area is backed by decades of scientific research.

"As we slow the brain wave patterns from beta to alpha to theta to delta, there is a corresponding increase in balance between the two hemispheres of the brain. This more balanced brain state is called brain synchrony, or brain synchronization."

"Whatever the technique [for meditating]," he continues, "the effect on the brain is substantially the same: synchronization of the two brain hemispheres - and after much practice, an experience of connection with the rest of the universe, accompanied by profound inner peace and happiness. Any kind of focusing will bring about a degree of brain synchronization. The greater the focus, the greater the synchronization, and the deeper the meditative state."

Really, all people are intuitive. We all have the ability to use our right brain, or our left brain, or both. It's simply that some have practiced this technique more than others and those that have are able to arrive at sound decisions more quickly, see the broader picture better, and employ both logic and creativity in their decision-making skills.

Cultivating your intuitive skills begins with acceptance. Accept that intuition exists and that you are an intuitive person, even if you've not yet learned to recognize it.

The next step is allowing. Allow yourself to slow down and tune in to your creative thoughts and feelings. Continue to bring forth information that you can learn from, and your skills and abilities will flow quite naturally.

"But, how do I know" you ask, "if what I receive is really intuitive information or just something my head made up?"

Good question and the answer is that the distinction can sometimes be subtle. There is a difference, but the distinctions are often quite fine. Don't let that discourage you, though. Invest time in practicing each day. If you do, you will find that your 'guesses' become more accurate. You will build confidence and self-trust. Continue practicing receipt of your intuition by accepting what you receive and trusting it. In time, as your intuition strengthens, you will come to know on your own the difference between intuition and 'your head'.

As you grow in your ability, you will know when to ask the 'bigger' questions that you feel are more important. You'll build confidence that when you ask . . . you *will* receive the answers intuitively. You will come to know that you *cannot not* receive.

As your intuition grows stronger and more reliable, begin to direct it in your day to day life. Use it in your decision making, in your creative leisure activities, in your work life, and anywhere else you can find to employ it.

Employing your intuition is also an excellent way to strengthen your spiritual sense of oneness with both the Creator and All That Is (a little side bonus, as if you needed one).

"Most of all, you are no longer in a hurry, because you are content in each moment even if you aren't 'there' yet (whatever that is for you). The inner journey is full of interest, full of rewards." ~ Bill Harris

Take time to slow down. Learn to tap into your intuition. You'll be glad you did.

I am inspired by the story of Film Producer and Director, Tracy Trost. Tracy hasn't always been in the film industry but directing feature films was a longtime dream of his that he has consciously brought to fruition.

"I own a direct mail marketing company," he says, "in the States. It's been a great company, a very successful company. I don't have any issues with it, except that it was not my dream. Since I met my wife, she's always asked me, 'Who are you and what do you want to be?' and I've always told her, 'One day I'll direct a major motion picture.'

It's always been a dream of mine, but I wasn't really doing anything to get there. I did television, but that's still not making films.

In my business I have about twelve employees and we do book meetings every month. We've read *Think and Grow Rich, Psychocybernetics,* and *As a Man Thinketh.* We've read all these great books together and when we meet I'll say to them, 'How can we apply the truth of this chapter to our lives?' I'm thinking first as an individual - how can I, Tracy Trost, apply the truth of this chapter to my life, and then as a company, how can I, Tracy Trost, apply the truth of this chapter to myself at Trost Consulting among the people I work with every day? Number three: How can we as a company apply the truth of this chapter to our customer relations?

So we were having one of these meetings and we were reading a book called *Release Your Brilliance* by Simon Bailey. It's a great book! And the chapter we were reading is about dreams. So I went around the room and said, 'If you could be anybody you wanted to be and if you could do that one thing that would define you (you'd say, 'this is what would make me who I am'), what would that one thing be?'

So I went around the room and one of the girls said, 'I've always wanted to be a masseuse. I've just always loved that type of work' and another of the girls said, 'I'd love to be a photographer. I love taking pictures and I would love that to be my life." Another girl said, I'd love to live in Colorado Springs, Colorado. I've always wanted to live there.' So we went around the room asking these questions and then I asked, 'Okay, so what are you doing on a daily basis to get there, because you have this thing that you say defines you and we know a trip doesn't happen by taking just one step. It takes planning, laying out a roadmap. What are you doing on a daily basis to get there?' And of course, they all look at you and they go, 'Nothing. We're working. I have my wife, a family . . .'

So what you need to do is start thinking, 'Here's my end goal. Here's where I am, so what do I need to do? Do I need to go to school?' Then go find a school and apply . . . train!

So then, one of the girls, her name is Melissa, looks at me and goes, 'Tracy, what is that one thing you would want to do? What would be your dream?'

'I can tell you that in two seconds. It's to direct movies, something I've always wanted to do. Something I've always said that I am, a director.'

So then she turned on me, 'So, what are you doing on a daily basis to get there?'"

Tracy starts laughing as he describes this next bit

"I said, 'You're fired. Get outta here! In fact, here's your ticket to Colorado! Bye!'"

I love Tracy's sense of humor, because, of course this last was told to me tongue-in-cheek through laughter. But obviously, it became a defining moment for him. Forced to look at his life's dream and what he had or had not so far achieved to realize it, he was also faced with a choice.

Trost continues: "I said, 'Melissa, you're right.' And I went home that night and I told my wife about this conversation and she asked, 'Why aren't you doing it? We've been married 21 years and this is something you've been going to do ever since I've known you. This is who you've always wanted to be. *What are you doing?*'

'You're right. I'm doing nothing. But I have a million excuses. I have a company to run, I have five children to take care of, a wife, a house, blah, blah, blah.'

And I realized, 'You know what? It's time to put your money where your mouth is. Just do it!'

So I started writing. And the first movie that we did was called *Find Me.* I started writing it that Christmas break and two years later we shot it over nine days with a bunch of help from my friends.

Since then, of the five film festivals we've entered into, it's taken first place with four, second in the fifth, and it won best actor in two other film festivals. So it's been a HUGE realization of a dream!

We just finished filming on our second movie, called *A Christmas Snow* and that'll be done in the fall [of 2010]."

When asked how he taps into his intuition to bring about such great projects, Tracy says, "For me, it's time alone . . . time in the morning, which currently is my jogging time, just to be quiet and just to think . . . do nothing more than think. I take time every day for this. Sometimes it's five minutes, sometimes it's an hour, it just depends on what it is. I get some of my best ideas when I do nothing more than think. I think of the possibilities. I think of 'what if'. Ideas come to me from God or Spirit and I quickly get out the recorder and say, 'This is what I need to do about this thing or that thing.'"

He also takes a similar approach to Bartmann and states, "Sometimes I will feed my subconscious and let it dwell on it. Sometimes I will give it something to think about while I sleep. That's when some of the best subconscious work is done."

Tracy offers the following advice for anyone wanting to pursue their dreams, "Take personal responsibility for your life. Stop blaming others for whatever's going on in your life. And just do it!

We are conscious creators. If you don't like where your life is going or what you've created, stop what you're doing and go a different direction. Start creating something else."

Tracy Trost says, "Think it, Say it, Do it! You can do it!"

Chapter Eight - The Way Forward

Men go abroad to wonder at the heights of mountains,
At the huge waves of the sea, at the long courses of the rivers,
At the vast compass of the ocean, at the circular motions of the
stars,
And they pass by themselves without wondering.
St Augustine

Well, it's been a good journey, one that I've thoroughly enjoyed sharing with you, and it's not over yet. In fact, now that you've rediscovered your passion, set some goals, created an action plan, worked on your motivation, identified possible hurdles, created laser-focus, and started to develop your intuition, I'd say your journey's just begun. I'm really excited for you, just knowing that you are now creating the life you've always wanted to live.

The beauty I see in you is that you have a great gift to share with this world and that the more you love and accept yourself, the more you inspire others to be whole and healthy and to live their dreams.

Martin Luther King, Jr. said, "The ultimate measure of a man is not where he stands in moments of comfort but where he stands at times of challenge and discovery."

This is that time. Will you measure up? Yes, you will, because it is your time to shine.

Now is the time for sharpening the saw, as Stephen R. Covey puts it . . . to continually improve yourself. Tony Robbins refers to this as CANI, the "constant and never-ending improvement" of the self. Great souls will always tell you that if you wish to live to your full potential, then you must constantly strive for improvement.

Now is the time for you to build a support network of like-minded people, people who either want the same things out of life that you do or will strongly support your goals anyway.

Tracy Trost states that, "When you put it to the Universe, 'This is who I want to be, this is what I want to do,' people will come to help you do what you need to do [to achieve your goal]." Now is the time to declare to the Universe, 'This is who I am and this is where I want to go in life.' Allow the Universe to work in your life by sending you aides and cheerleaders to help you get to where you want to be.

Now is the time for clearing your mind of chatter and to learn to meditate, for focusing your mind in a single, purposeful direction.

And now is the time to change the way you used to think . . . to clear out those last vestiges of limiting beliefs. The Buddha in The Dhammapada said, "Our life is shaped by our mind. We become what we think." *Above all else,* this will be the key to whether or not you succeed in living your dreams.

Lynne McTaggart tells of a scientific experiment that proves exactly this point. She states, "The Intention Experiment rests on an outlandish premise; thought affects physical reality. A sizable body of research exploring the nature of consciousness, carried on for more than 30 years in prestigious scientific institutions around the world, shows that thoughts are capable of affecting everything from the simplest machines to the most complex living beings.

This evidence suggests that human thoughts and intentions are an actual physical 'something' with the astonishing power to change our world. Every thought we have is a tangible energy with the power to transform. A thought is not only a thing; a thought is a thing that influences other things."

Epictetus said that "We cannot choose our external circumstances, but we can always choose how we respond to them" and after years in a Nazi concentration camp, seeing those he loved and cared about tortured and killed in the most horrific of manners, Viktor Frankl determined exactly the same thing.

He said, "Everything can be taken from a man but one thing; the last of the human freedoms - to choose one's attitude in any given set of circumstances, to choose one's own way."

Swami Chidananda believed firmly "that a man's destiny is in his own hands" and that "he shall depend upon himself. He is the one to decide on the pattern of the experience to come. He is the master of his destiny. He is the architect of his fate. He has nothing to fear in this universe, nothing except his own wrong actions and thoughts."

If you are of the Christian faith, you may have heard your pastor tell you last Sunday that, in the Bible, Jesus also admonished us to guard our thoughts when he said, "Finally, brothers, whatever is true, whatever is noble, whatever is right, whatever is pure, whatever is lovely, whatever is admirable - if anything is excellent or praiseworthy - think about such things" because it is in so doing that we direct our subconscious minds to bring us more of those things, instead of the things that we do not want.

Marcus Aurelius was a strong proponent of guarding and changing the way you think. He said in his Meditations, "Your mind will be like its habitual thoughts; for the soul becomes dyed with the color of its thoughts. Soak it then in such trains of thoughts as, for example: Where life is possible at all, a right life is possible."

He came to the same conclusions that Epictetus and Frankl did, saying that "if you are distressed by anything external, the pain is not due to the thing itself but to your own estimate of it and this you have the power to revoke at any moment."

Burt Goldman tells a story which illustrates well the power of choice:

> The incident took place during a class I was presenting. I was heading out to lunch at a nearby restaurant with 3 of my students, and offered to drive. As we approached my new car, we saw a big dent in the right front fender.
>
> Someone had slammed into it while it was parked, and had driven off without even leaving a note on the windshield. The three students looked at me and waited for the blowup.
>
> When I first saw that dented fender, my mind flew off into all kinds of directions. For a moment I could feel irritation and my body tightening with anger, and I knew immediately I had to redirect that negative mental activity at once. I used the Energy Redirection Technique and focused on finding a way to **change the negative thoughts into positive action**.
>
> Jumping into the car I said to the three, "Let's go. There's a body and fender shop just down the street." "You going to get it fixed right now?" One of the students asked.
>
> "Nope." I answered, "What I'm going to do is to get a price on what it costs to repair the dent, and whatever that price turns out to be, **I'm going to create something that I'm not doing right now, and I'm going to make three times the cost of the dent**."

We drove to a nearby shop and I was told that the cost of repairing the fender would be $450.00. I immediately tripled the figure and thought, "$1,350, I've got to earn $1,350.00 with something new."

Now whenever I looked at the dent in my fender I didn't mentally start cursing the low life who dented it and ran off. No, not at all. Now when I looked at the dent I thought, "$1,350.00, I've got to earn $1,350.00."

I kept thinking of how I could make that amount of money. It had to be something that I was not doing at that time. I put on my Creative Hat and thought about it, and finally came up with the answer.

I would create a brand new seminar for my friends and if they liked it I would send out a mailing to all the people who had been through my classes, and would set a goal of making $1,350.00 from it!

And so I put the seminar together and did it for free-of-charge for fifteen friends. They loved it. I then sent out a mailing and conducted the new seminar.

Imagine my surprise when I realized that I had made more on that seminar than the new car cost! And all because someone dented my fender.

We all go through unpleasant circumstances at times and we all, occasionally, have fleeting thoughts of a negative or unhelpful nature. But what do we do with them? Do we dismiss them like Goldman, letting them go without so much as a second thought along the same line? Better yet, like both Johnson and Goldman, do we take the opportunity to turn negative thoughts and situations into positive opportunities? Or do we dwell upon them until they fester in a swamp of putrefied negative? Carlos Castaneda says, "The trick is in what one emphasizes."

It may be a challenge and as Bill Harris said, "personal evolution takes time and work," but I have full faith that you can and will rise to that challenge.

Mary Anne Radmacher said that "Courage doesn't always roar. Sometimes courage is the quiet voice at the end of the day saying, 'I will try again tomorrow.'"

If you stumble in your efforts, so what? No need to berate yourself or think yourself a failure. Simply pick yourself up, dust yourself off and, more determined than ever before, take up the mantle to carry on again until you succeed!

Castaneda says, "The basic difference between an ordinary man and a warrior is that a warrior takes everything as a challenge." Don your warrior gear and be ready to do battle with your old habitual way of thinking. Emerge, perhaps battle-scarred, but victorious, a new and better you, one who is ready and willing to live up to his or her full potential and shine brightly for all the world to see.

Brian Johnson, a man who thoroughly enjoys living his passions, said, "You want to give light? (I certainly hope that answer is an unequivocal 'YES!!') Then you must endure the burning. You must endure the challenges of discovering who you are and how you're going to fit into this world, let alone really LIVE in this world. How you're going to trek out into the forest of your own hero's journey again and again and again. Each time facing your demons and coming back to the world with your gifts. Again and again and again. It's not going to be 'easy.' But who wants that anyway? Remember, we're no longer looking for a way to discharge our tension at any cost - we're looking for a goal worthy of us . . . a goal that sets us on fire and lights our splendid torches!!! Right?!?"

I will leave you with one final thought from the illustrious author, Dr. Seuss. In his fun and famous rhyming fashion, he said, "You have brains in your head. You have feet in your shoes. You can steer yourself any direction you choose. And will you succeed? Yes indeed, yes indeed! Ninety-eight and three-quarters percent guaranteed."

You won't realize the distance you've walked until you take a look around and realize how far you've been. ~ Anon.

BIBLIOGRAPHY

Allen, Deborah. *Just Can't Do Without Your Twin.* Twins Realm, Stories From and About Other Twins, http://www.twinsrealm. com/othr_txt.html. 07 March 2010

Andrews, B. *It is Unnerving Knowing She Can See What I am Envisioning.* True Psychic Stories - Telepathy, http://www. truepsychicstories.com/category/telepathy/. 07 March 2010.

Bartmann, Bill. Personal Interview, 22 April 2010.

Ben-Shahar, Tal. *Happier.* New York; McGraw Hill Books, 2007.

Canfield, Jack and Mark Victor Hansen. *Dare to Win.* New York; The Berkley Publishing Group, 1994.

Castaneda, Carlos. *The Wheel of Time.* New York; Washington Square Press, 2001.

Csikszentmihalyi, Mihalyi. *Flow.* New York; Harper Collins Publishers, 1991.

Cohen, Andrew. *The Law of Karma.* EnlightenNext Magazine, 04 March 2010.

Covey, Stephen R. *The 7 Habits of Highly Effective People.* New York; Free Press, 2004.

DeMoss, Mark. *The Little Red Book of Wisdom.* Nashville, Tennessee; Thomas Nelson, Inc. 2007.

Eker, T. Harv. *Secrets of the Millionaire Mind.* New York; Harper Collins Publishing, 2005.

Fisher, Glenn. Personal Interview, 26 February 2010.

Hajee, Karim. *How to Develop Your Intuition.* http://www.self-esteem-and-confidence-improvement.com/intuition.htm. 07 March 2010.

Hameroff, Stuart and Roger Penrose. *The Quantum Origins of Consciousness, EnlightenNext* magazine. Jun-Aug 2010.

Harms, Ernest., *Origins of Modern Psychiatry*, Thomas 1967 ASIN: B000NR852U.

Harris, Bill. *Thresholds of the Mind: Your Personal Roadmap to Success, Happiness, and Contentment.* Centerpointe Research Institute, Beaverton, Oregon, 2007.

Johnson, Brian. Personal Interview, 26 March 2010.

Johnson, Donna. *Use Your Intuition as Your Guide. http://www.djcsfirm.com/articles/PDFs/intuition.pdf.* 06 March 2010

Jung, Andrea. Goldsea Asian American Wonder Women. http://www.goldsea.com/WW/Jungandrea/jungandrea.html, 20 February 2010.

Lee, Bruce. Gaia Community, http://www.gaia.com/quotes/topics/flexibility#ixzz0g687Wu0K, 20 February 2010.

MacArthur, Cecily. Personal Interview, 22 April 2010.

Maltz, Maxwell. 1968 Interview with Betsy David. http://www.youtube.com/watch?v=AUbK0nql64c, 27 February 2010.

Maltz, Maxwell. *Psycho-Cybernetics.* New York; Pocket Books, 1969.

Miller, Earl K. *Cognitive Control: Understanding the Brain's Executive.*
Lecture at Massachusetts Institute of Technology, 12 June 2003.

McCoy Jr., Charles W. *Why Didn't I Think of That? Think the Unthinkable and Achieve Creative Greatness.* Paramus, New Jersey; Prentice Hall Press, 2002.

McTaggart, Lynne. *The Intention Experiment: Use your Thoughts to Change the World.* London; Harper Element, 2007.

McTaggart, Lynne. *The Field.* London; HarperCollins, 2001.

McVoy, Jeanette. Personal Interview, 26 February 2010.

Parashar, Avish. *Dealing With Flat Tires on the Path to Success,* Email to the Author, 07/13/2011.

Proctor, Bob. *The Science of Getting Rich, http://www. thesgrprogram.com/online/lessons/2-lawofattraction,* 20 *February 2010.*

Rifenbary, Jay. *No Excuse!* Hummelstown, PA; Possibility Press, 2007.

Robinson, Sir Ken. (23rd June 2009) "TED Talks: Schools Kill Creativity", Training Zone, http://www.trainingzone.co.uk/topic/ted-talk-schools-kill-creativity, 07 February 2010.

Schwendener, Shari Repasz. *128 Program April 2005. http:// www.gravityarts.org/media/128%20Program%20v3%20 view%20order.pdf.* 07 March 2010.

Seligman, Martin. *Learned Optimism.* New York; Pocket Books, 1998.

Simpson, Stephen. *Confidence.* (audio version) Published by Tony Wrighton, 2009.

Silva, Jose and Burt Goldman. *The Silva Mind Control Method of Mental Dynamics.*

Pocket Books, New York, 1998.

Stovall, Jim. Personal interview, 01 May 2010.

Stovall, Jim. *Christopher's Story*. http://www.jimstovall.com/. 01 May 2010.

Stovall, Jim. *What I Look for in a Coach*. Teleconference, Viki Winterton, host. 07 January 2010.

Trost, Tracy J. Personal Interview, 03 May 2010.

Vallortigara G, Rogers LJ. (2005). *Survival With an Asymmetrical Brain: Advantages and Disadvantages of Cerebral Lateralization*. Behav Brain Sci.28(4):575 - 89.

Walsch, Neale Donald. *Conversations With God*. New York; The Penguin Group, 2005.

Walsch, Neale Donald. *The New Revelations*. New York; Atria Books, 2002.

Wikipedia. The Psychoanalytic Unconscious. http://psychology. wikia.com/wiki/Unconscious_mind. 14 May 2010.

Zipern, Karen. (18 December 2004) *Fleeting Images of Fearful Faces Reveal Neurocircuitry of Unconscious Anxiety*, Medical News Today, http://www.medicalnewstoday.com/articles/18022.php, 20 February 2010.